T0083518

Karolinum Press

MODERN CZECH CLASSICS

Jiří Pelán
Bohumil Hrabal
A Full-Length Portrait

Translated from the Czech by David Short

KAROLINUM PRESS 2019

KAROLINUM PRESS
Karolinum Press is a publishing department of Charles University
Ovocný trh 560/5, 116 36 Prague 1
Czech Republic
www.karolinum.cz

Text © 2019 by Jiří Pelán
Translation and notes © 2019 by David Short
Photographs © Václav Chochola – heirs, Emanuel Frynta – heirs, Jiří Kolář –
heirs, c/o Dilia, Milan Jankovič – heirs, Tomáš Mazal, Jan Reich, 2019

Designed by Zdeněk Ziegler
Set and printed in the Czech Republic by Karolinum Press
First English edition

Cataloguing-in-Publication Data is available from the National Library
of the Czech Republic

ISBN 978–80–246–3909–3 (pb)
ISBN 978–80–246–3950–5 (epub)

CONTENTS

I

When Bohumil Hrabal's *Poupata* (Flower Buds) appeared in 1970, the few lucky souls who managed to lay hands on copies that had escaped the shredder and who had missed the previously published extracts from the long narrative poem *Bambino di Praga*, discovered to their surprise that Hrabal, a remarkable story-teller, had started out as a poet, that a writer, whose prose was typified by its flawless osmosis with what was most coarse-grained, venomous and ruthless about everyday life, had toyed, as he embarked on his writing career, with slightly off-beat semantic configurations to create some ornately impressionistic "Art nouveau tinkerings in verse".[1]

Today, Hrabal's oeuvre having been brought to a definitive conclusion, it would obviously be a grave error to see in this early verse (first assembled as a whole in its original form in the volume *Básnění* [Versifying] as part of the 1992 Collected Works edition, that is, *SSBH* in the Literature) mere juvenile experiments that at best document an adolescent yen to write and are touching testimony to their author's misguidedly high rating of his own talent. These lyrical beginnings are in fact extraordinarily important to any understanding of Hrabal's poetics – and his "literary destiny" generally; and given that, in *Flower Buds*, Hrabal went back to them later, as a writer who had already made a name for himself (though with numerous other texts still hidden away in old folders and bottom drawers), he was undoubtedly aware of their importance himself.

Even at this early stage, what we are seeing is a need – if in an adolescent, mildly graphomanic form – to write out of his system everything that was his life at the time, to put into words all "the dreaming, the platonic love-making, the student boozing, and the endless walks in shades of pink and gold".[2] From the very start of his career, writing was more important to Hrabal than living: the poet and translator Kamil Bednář and the critic, art theorist and

---

1) Bohumil Hrabal: 'Doslov' [Afterword] to *Poupata: Křehké a rabiátské texty z let 1938-1952* [Flower buds: Delicate and disorderly texts from the period 1938-1952], Prague: Mladá fronta, 1970, p. 237. Also as: *Kdo jsem*, in the Collected Works edition (hereafter abbreviated to *SSBH* and volume no., see Literature herein, p. 91), Vol. 12, p. 303.
2) Ibid.

translator Karel Teige did try to put him off writing, but he never stopped, writing on and on, as if racing against time. If Pirandello's "la vita o si vive o si scrive" is broadly true, it applies doubly to this early Hrabal.

Hrabal's life was absorbed to the last drop by his literature; by nature he was timid, and, constantly pursued by his "total fears",[3] the ground beneath his feet never firm, he had to force himself into contact with life by prescribing "artificial destinies" to himself and casting himself in roles (of, say, a labourer or insurance agent) that were not even remotely cut to the measure of his disposition. His position in life was that of an observer and – as he reiterated constantly – a *recorder*: throughout, his task was to record images from life, whether they sprang up before his gaze or rose out of stories told by others. He "wrote" those moments with the same intensity with which others lived them; and the moment he felt that he had "recorded" everything, he lost interest in living.

This obsession, this need, to make every transient image gleam with a new presence, is, by its nature, lyrical. Hrabal had not been wrong about his particular talent: if, following his juvenile overture, he turned to prose, we are entitled to believe that this switch, too, was a considered decision, one of the imposed "artificial destinies" that were to bring him closer to a life in anarchy. But then his prose never did displace this lyrical foundation: on the contrary, the horizontal of the narrative segments in his short stories is constantly intersected by the vertical of lyrical expression. Later developments merely confirmed that, for him, the lyrical and narrative modes were freely interchangeable. It is no accident that during his phase of "total realism", when he produced such a superlative narrative text as *Jarmilka*, he also wrote – now in the same total-realist diction – two spectacular poems, *Krásná Poldi* (Poldi the Beautiful Steelworks) and *Bambino di Praga*. And a particularly eloquent example of the unity between the two poles in Hrabal's work is the fact that the first version of *Příliš hlučná samota* (Too Loud a Solitude), the acme of his work in the 1980s, was also written in verse.

As with all juvenilia, Hrabal's early poems were in search of models, paradigms, that would help his particular sensibility to speak

---

3) A key idea that will peak as the title of one of Hrabal's late prose pieces. [DS]

out and put his own sensory experiences in some kind of order. He was to recall later, on numerous occasions, how, back then, he had read everything that he could lay his hands on. While it may be banal to say that the emancipation of any author's voice comes about against the backdrop of literature that has gone before, it is no less true that this dialogue with the polyphony of literary texts unfolds in manners unique to each and every author. In Hrabal's case, it has to be stressed, this period of intense dialogue with existing literature overlapped almost entirely with the first period of his output (from the lyrical verse of the 1940s to the prose of the 1950s); back then he was in permanent "communication with literature",[4] and it was then that he discovered all the writers that he would later acknowledge time and time again: Ungaretti, Céline, Schopenhauer, Nietzsche, Kafka, Chekhov, Babel, Faulkner and, above all, his Czech forerunners Jaroslav Hašek, Ladislav Klíma and Jakub Deml. Later on, he did very little reading: he gave his pantheon its final form at quite an early stage, and although he never stopped dropping these names, with fervour and respect, to the very last, this was more born of a disciple's gratitude than it constituted a body of developing, constantly updated, attitudes. The moment Hrabal found his own poetics he patently lost all interest in reading as a corrective to the direction in which he was going: he had not the slightest intention of keeping pace with the literary trends of the day, he lacked any kind of competitive instinct and was not interested in being "up-to-date", and nothing was more alien to him than strategic musings on the current state of the book market (unlike many others setting out on a writing career in the 1960s). Accordingly, intertextuality researches never arrive at a more than a very limited body of palimpsests. And therein probably lies one reason for the surprising fact that, though whole decades could pass between the writing of so many of Hrabal's works and their appearance in print, this has never been a particular obstacle to their reception.

Hrabal's persistent references to his great icons is indicative of something at least for the first phase of his career. He tells us himself of the extraordinary importance to his poetic beginnings of Ungaretti (more precisely the Ungaretti of *Il porto sepolto* [The

4) *SSBH*, Vol. 17, p. 308.

buried port, 1916], Czech translation by Zdeněk Kalista, 1934, that is, the Ungaretti associated with pre-war avant-garde Modernism), and of Czech Poetism and Surrealism.

Ungaretti's being named in the role of Hrabal's teacher has generally been rather perplexing: the lyrical concentration of Ungaretti's texts has been seen as the complete antithesis of the somewhat disorderly rambling of Hrabal's works in prose, encircling reality *ad infinitum* with ever new imagery. However, if we can dismiss such comparing and contrasting as merely superficial, the trigger effect of Ungaretti's verse is actually quite conclusive:[5] while in Hrabal's early poems we may find no quotations from or allusions to *Il porto sepolto*, many of them genuinely come close to the Ungarettian verse of hints and pauses that apprehends the world of objects in simultaneous perceptions expressed in sober language:

> I want to go to sleep. But see!
> A cart flows silently down the sliced-open street
> like a barge along a navigation
> and the horses,
> two brown blots,
> row to the rhythm of their nodding necks,
> while the counterpoint
> of a shower of sobbing drums away from boredom.[6]

Hrabal's verse, too, like Ungaretti's, aspires at this stage to be a "concentrated footprint of emotional life" and "beautiful biography". Hrabal's verse, too, seeks to speak in "essential" metaphors, and, above all, Hrabal's verse, too, desires to go beyond being mere ornament, to touch the existential horizon and to speak of those rare moments when the individual dissolves into the whole, becoming one "docile thread of the universe":

> A slumbering village
> was smouldering

5) For another closely argued view of the Hrabal-Ungaretti connection see David Chirico: 'Towards a Typology of Hrabal's Intertextuality: Bohumil Hrabal and Giuseppe Ungaretti', in Short: *Bohumil Hrabal*, pp. 11–33.
6) *Město v dešti* (The City in the Rain), in *SSBH*, Vol. 1, p. 85 (trans. DS).

with happiness,
the monotonous barking of dogs counted
the hours
and a chugging train shattered
the fragrant dark,
galloping somewhere across the land like
a copper stallion.
Bewitched, still in the small hours I was
sipping
from the goblet of night until I had left
at the bottom
only
dew-decked stars.[7]

Not for nothing have we placed such emphasis here on the Ungarettian roots of Hrabal's juvenile verse: the main reason is that many shades of inspiration from that source later crop up as key components of Hrabal's mature prose. One of his guiding principles will continue to be the search for "essential images", and one fundamental reason for him to write will always be the urge to record sudden, intuitive perceptions of a vital depth and fullness (a meaning that can also be attached to his familiar metaphor of the *perlička na dně* – variously translated as 'a/the [little] pearl on *or* at the bottom' [of a tale]).[8]

From this perspective it can also be appreciated why Hrabal, in a single breath, spoke not just of the lesson of Ungaretti, but also of that of Poetism and Surrealism (he actually said that he hoped to initiate – in collaboration with his friend Karel Marysko – a trend to be called "Neopoetism"). For Poetism, which emerged at the very start of the 1920s as a product of the Czech adoption of European avant-garde verse (notably the Cubist patterns of associative combination initiated by Apollinaire's *Zone* [1912]), and the programme of which was given concrete form by nearly two dozen poets, prose-writers, dramatists and artists (Karel Teige, Vítězslav

7) *Scherzo*, in *SSBH*, Vol. 1, p. 136 (trans. DS).
8) The short-story collection *Perlička na dně* remains untranslated into English. A film version exists whose traditional English title is *Pearls of the Deep* (1965), which translation will be kept in later references to the book. [DS]

Nezval, Jaroslav Seifert, Konstantin Biebl, Vladislav Vančura, Adolf Hoffmeister among others), sought above all else to magic life itself into words: life as an unpredictable adventure, life in its simultaneous manifestations – beyond the hierarchy of high and low, life as data presented directly to the senses, and life in its lyrical immediacy. The instrument of this two-way permeation of life and poetry, the principle of association, an instrument common to Poetism and Surrealism, again points to the core method that Hrabal applies to his prose: the multidimensional evocation of reality by means of juxtaposed images. The poetics of both Cubism (Reverdy) and Surrealism (Breton) recommended bringing closer together the most mutually distant realities (Reverdy: "The more distant and clear-cut the relations between two realities that have been drawn together, the more powerful will an image be and the greater its emotive force and poetic reality."[9]), and Hrabal the prose-writer, speaking in one Babelesque breath of "a diamond and gonorrhoea",[10] was unshakeably steadfast in his application of the principle.

For its part, Hrabal's attitude to Surrealism is rather complex. It is broadly the case that the prose Hrabal – like so many modern European prose-writers – happily exploits the prodigious expansion of the space made available to the imagination by the Surrealist experience. In particular his tendency to transform the real through hyperbole is indubitably the fruit of this Surrealist dauntlessness. Yet Hrabal's relation to Surrealism is in no way circumscribed by this vague legacy. He was obviously also fascinated by the Surrealist practice of *écriture automatique*; and while this fascination is projected in his early verse with moderation, it is much more in evidence – in a modified form – in his only slightly later interest in the unregulated stream of narration based on "oral gesture", and then again in the 1970s, after he has given up on his compositional method of ex post collage, favouring instead writing "alla prima". To this extent, then, Hrabal's recurrently vaunted attachment to

9) Pierre Reverdy, *Le gant de crin* (1927), in: Idem, *Oeuvres complètes* II, ed. Étienne-Alain Hubert, Paris: Flammarion, 2010, p. 555: "Plus les rapports des deux réalités rapprochées seront lointains et justes, plus l'image sera forte, plus elle aura de puissance émotive et de réalité poétique."
10) See, for example, 'Interview na hrázi věčnosti' (An interview on the dike of eternity), in *Domácí úkoly* (*SSBH*, Vol. 15), p. 269.

Surrealism is more to do with method than content. There is, for example, one disparity in the fact that Hrabal's "flow" method, clearly an echo of Surrealist automatism, is far from conceding a core role to the unconscious (the dream records of 1944 are a mere episode) and is not a pathway to oneiric alternative worlds; on the contrary, it remains – more in line with the Cubist tradition – totally tied to the crudest of reality and its supply of the verbal "ready made". This typical contradiction need not, however, be made too much of, since the way Czech Surrealism evolved did rather blunt it: there is no overlooking the fact that in the 1940s and 1950s the second wave of Czech Surrealism (Zbyněk Havlíček, Karel Hynek, Oldřich Wenzl) admitted solid chunks of the specific (including politically anchored) reality into the imaginative space while also intellectualising its methods (notably through humour, sarcasm and irony).

II

It has often been averred that the most remarkable period in Hrabal's development was the 1950s. And yet this time of workshop trials remained long hidden from view. Hrabal made his debut in 1956 with *Hovory lidí* (Things People Say, a bibliophile edition of 250 copies), coming to the notice of a wider public only in 1963, by then as a seasoned author with a distinctive style, through the collection *Pearls of the Deep*.[11] The first insight into the work that pre-dated these publications came with his personal anthology *Flower Buds* (1970), while a broader view can be gleaned from two volumes of his Collected Works: Vol. 2, *Židovský svícen* (Menorah, 1991) and Vol. 3, *Jarmilka* ([a girl's name], 1992).

The 1948 Communist coup, which cast Czechoslovakia out of its short-lived and shaky phase of post-war democracy right into an era that was the acme of Stalinism, meant a second break in the evolution of Czech culture (the first had been occasioned by Nazi occupation), and an extraordinarily brutal one at that. Many major writers, such as Egon Hostovský, Jan Čep, Milada Součková and Ivan Blatný, emigrated, some forty writers, including Jan Zahradníček, Zdeněk Rotrekl, Zdeněk Kalista, Josef Palivec, Jiří Mucha and Josef Knap, disappeared for many years into the country's jails, while Záviš Kalandra was executed. Avant-garde modernism was rejected; its erstwhile representatives, all of them left-leaning, fell prey to persecution (Teige, Biebl), opted unwillingly for silence (Seifert), or adapted their poetics to order (Nezval). Most literary journals were extinguished, foreign literature was prevented from entering the country, mountains of recent publications were turned into waste paper and thousands of titles were removed from libraries. The publishing plans of the newly nationalised houses were trimmed radically back to a narrow "cultural legacy" (what were called "progressive" classics) to serve as the backdrop against which a new literature might emerge, offering a positive and optimistic image of the path newly taken towards "bright tomorrows". The total devaluation of aesthetic criteria meant that second- and third-rate authors donned the mantle of representing Czech literature.

11) See note 8. [DS]

All connection with post-war developments in the West was not totally eliminated. In fact, even the officially sanctioned output – prose lauding partisans, collectivisation and the construction of socialism and verse panegyrics on the new idols and ideals (from the pens of such as Jan Drda, Václav Řezáč, Bohumil Říha, Pavel Kohout or Milan Kundera), all manufactured in line with instructions laid down by Andrei Aleksandrovich Zhdanov – ran largely in parallel to the general post-war revaluation of politically or ethically engaged literature, as represented by, for example, the Sartre-esque novel or Italian Neorealism. In the Czech context, however, the specific feature of this trend was that the texts published were typically highly schematic ideologically and went for a long time without any polemical counterpoint, such as the western literary context soon had in Beckett's immoralism, Robbe-Grillet's apathetic stock-taking of physical objects or mental acts, Queneau's non-mimetic construc- tions or Calvino's use of allegory. Such correctives only started to pass into Czech culture with the gradual de-Stalinisation of cultural politics, and the great depth of the crisis that had to be gradually overcome was tempered, from the later 1950s onwards, by some relaxation of the previously severe publishing plans, including the role that came to be played, as alternatives to Socialist Realism, by certain *engagé* texts of western provenance, for example, writings by Alberto Moravia, Pier Paolo Pasolini or Italo Calvino.

If we confine our considerations to published texts only, the impression is left that Czech culture was quite untouched by the explosion of creative energies, stalled by the war, which made themselves felt during the 1950s in other European literatures and gave rise to numerous innovations in both prose and verse while quickly making earlier, highly conservative engagé literature look quite antiquated. This view is necessarily false, since we can only form a true image of 1950s literary output in Czech by bringing in not only the – often fairly dull – work produced in exile, but, and above all, the vast body of writings engendered either within closed circles of friends or in total isolation, and with no hope of their ever being published.

Such writings, including many by Hrabal, never actually lost contact with what was going on throughout European post-war literature, and since their authors were aware that publication was impossible, they were, paradoxically, amazingly liberated and full of adventurous explorations. They eventually began to reach a wider public during the 1960s, and a major part of the remarkable creativity of the time is attributable precisely to these delayed publications. For a complete and reliable mapping of the subterranean continent created in the 1950s, so heterogeneous as to the subjects and means of expression employed back then, we had to wait until the 1990s and the new situation in the politics of culture that arose after the fall of Communism. Thus, viewed in retrospect, Hrabal's samizdat production of the 1950s proves to be among the most important items that had been passed by. *En passant*, let us also mention here such other crucial items as, among others, the hermetic lyrical and existentialist narrative verse of Vladimír Holan, the civilisation poetry of Jiří Kolář, inspired by Sandburg and Lee Masters, the spiritual meditations of Jan Zahradníček, the verse of Bohuslav Reynek, imbued with a Franciscan humility, the rudimentary autobiographical fragments of Jan Hanč, the introspective probing of Jiřina Hauková, the concrete surrealism of Zbyněk Havlíček and the ironic surrealism of Karel Hynek, the mystical spirituality of Jan Kameník, the brutish naïvisme of Egon Bondy, the uniquely humour-infused "embarrassing poetry" of Ivo Vodseďálek and the jazz prose of Josef Škvorecký.

It was natural that Hrabal, who even in his juvenile lyrical verse aspired to testify to life's authenticity (and at the end of his life he declared that a writer's basic disposition is "amazement at the visible world"[12]), could not accept the schematic parameters laid down by the Stalinist culture policy in force at the time. But then he did not have the slightest reason to: for him, writing was always an elemental, inner need, a thoroughly personal task bordering on egotism; throughout the 1940s and 1950s he wrote without regard to any readership. Writing the foreword to *Utrpení starého Werthera* (The Sorrows of Old Werther, 1981) in an evocation of those times, he said: "It was never me anywhere, it was all the others, things beyond me, I saw myself as no more than a pocket mirror…".[13] And later still, as he took stock, he would keep repeating that writing

---

12) *Beseda v restauraci Hájenka* (A conversazione in the Hájenka restaurant), in *SSBH*, Vol. 17, pp. 268–300 (268).
13) *SSBH*, Vol. 2, p. 239.

for him had never been anything other than "an exchange of love letters" with the world,[14] a lovelorn gaze fixed on "nature", "the human milieu", "all those veins and strata of human life",[15] and "a running commentary on reality, sort of progressing from minute to minute, day to day".[16]

As a "recorder" – never a "writer" – he was basically untouched by the imperatives of the cultural ideology of the age. True, by the end of the 1940s his writing, which had begun in a spirit of expressionism, was increasingly consciously borne along by the idea of mimesis; however, this mimesis was equally *désengagé* and free from all pragmatic considerations. What interested him were not ideological disputes over the complexion of literature, but Aristotelian "nature". To the extent that the Hrabal of the early 1950s turned instinctively to where this "nature" manifested itself in elementary, plebeian, forms, this did not constitute a turning away *from* literature: on the contrary, this was for him the only thinkable route *to* literature. This was the road to "total realism" (the term he was to borrow later from his friend Egon Bondy), a non-ideological, apolitical, non-didactic realism, in a sense even an amoral realism. Paradoxically, of course, this radically apolitical stance made Hrabal the most authentic chronicler of the 1950s (and obviously not just of that decade) and gave his texts *in retrospect* an unmistakably political dimension.

Hrabal himself, writing an afterword to *Flower Buds* in the late 1970s, was surprised at the instinctive consequentiality of the choices he had made:

> I even invented a theory to account for me, the theory of "artificial destiny", sticking my own self somewhere I never wanted to be. I, shy little me, used to hawk life insurance, was an assistant in a pharmacy, had a job at a steelworks, but always I kept on writing. The bleak, coarse side of reality came whooshing towards me, blinding me like a blizzard. And I, instead of dreaming and reflecting, I took a great liking to reality just as it was.[17]

14) *Beseda*, p. 273.
15) Ibid.
16) Ibid., p. 270.
17) *Poupata*, p. 237. Also in *SSBH*, Vol. 12, pp. 303–304.

Hrabal repeated the choice made by his beloved Isaak Babel, a timid intellectual who, in search of reality, had cast himself into the brutal turmoil of civil war; the similarities between their poetics is entirely due to that gesture. Having spent the last years of the war as a train dispatcher at Kostomlaty (thereafter completing his legal studies to graduate in 1946), he had then been an insurance agent for the *Starobní a invalidní živnostenský fond* (Tradesmen's Old-age and Invalidity Fund, 1945–47), a rep for a wholesale company (1947–48), a volunteer at the Kladno iron and steel works (1949–53), an employee of the state enterprise in charge of recycling (1954–59) and a stagehand at one of the Prague theatres (1959–61). Each of these environments provided Hrabal with an endless stock of material, observed and recorded by his "eidetic memory", whether that material was the product of his own postmortemising or had been provided by the "things people say". The key problem of his work at this time was how to apprehend and organise the material, how to furnish this raw content with a literary syntax. The struggle to find a personal poetics had been particularly intense back in the early 1950s (the core years were actually 1949–52), but by the time the struggle was over all the constituents of his poetics were firmly in place.

III

The main observable tendency during this period is Hrabal's quest for some balance between the lyrical basis of his vision (enchantment, amazement, an indestructible longing for Plato's "begetting in the beautiful") and the brutality of the prose of life that each new milieu afforded him. The job had to be tackled repeatedly, and the different solutions constituted the alternative styles that would, in most cases, resurface later on in Hrabal's career as a writer.

Lyrical enthusiasm is still the driving force of the collection *Židovský svícen* (Menorah, typescript of 1949), which contains seven shorter stories and the longer "existential short-story" 'Kain' (Cain, on which more anon). However, the raw material for these stories already consists largely of hyperbolised narrative segments that draw on specific environments (a railway station, a brewery) and on "things people say", here the discourse of two cynical insurance agents who blithely have a dying man sign a contract. This time, the lyrical tension is regulated consistently by a grammatical operation: all these shorter texts are presented in the second-person plural (i.e. the 'you' form). The subjective, lyrical *Ich* is concealed behind the "you" that belongs formally to the objective, storybook universe that is being evoked. In fact, however, this "you" is a point of intersection from which one can equally well set off in pursuit of the story being told or of its lyrical transformation, it being the wellspring as much of narrative distance as of lyrical empathy.

Thus, for example: one of the best pieces in the collection is the short story 'Dům, který se osvěžoval bleskem' (The House that was Refreshed by Lightning), of which the narrative bare bones are this: a stationmaster's wife falls pregnant just as she is leaning out of the window, waving to her departing mother, her husband having jumped her from behind without warning; the little girl born of this momentary union listens, enchanted, to her father's descriptions of the universe; in time the stationmaster goes mad, rubberstamps his own entire body and commits suicide; his wife lives out the rest of her life in an asylum. The story is also undoubtedly remarkable for its existentialist "gory-story" dimension, so typical of the later Hrabal – with eros and thanatos as the fateful bounds of human freedom; however, we only mention that here in order to illustrate how the grammatical "you" opens up, above the narrative segments, a space for breathtaking lyrical elegy:

> Surely you can remember that afternoon, station master! That glorious afternoon that everyone for miles around remembers. It's still not coming back. You're too remote from us, but maybe you'll remember how you uncovered the Burdensome Death file as if you knew where it sprang from. You came to the very jaws of your doom (or salvation?)! And you sucked that curse up into the tiniest of your blood vessels. Put better: you set your imprint against the matrix! You matched your teacher, your master! You found your God! Your everything! And having locked yourself in your office, you stripped naked and stamped your body all over with all the rubber stamps you used to use. In all the inks, so after half an hour's meticulous endeavour you looked like a gigantic parrot! For your rear you contrived a device from a poker and some string and a pair of sugar tongs so that even your back got its fair share! So not a single spot got left out! And then you took a tiny revolver with a mother-of-pearl grip and shot yourself in the temple. (...) ... anyone who seeks causes and works them out from effects will confirm that it was a neat job by Burdensome Death! The same Burdensome Death that is glad for a certain lady in an asylum to lean twice a day from a first-floor window, though it's actually happening on the ground floor, from where she is waving good-bye to her departing mother, albeit the latter has been dead for several years. It's the Burdensome Death that was happy for the lady to fall pregnant twice a day, though she was long past the menopause.[18]

Thus this first step on the way to prose gave rise to a poetics of which the characteristic feature is the ambivalence of the narrator, perched as he is between lyrical subjectivity and story-telling objectivity. At the turn of the 1940s and 1950s, this ambivalence became so assertive as the guiding principle of Hrabal's writing that it also impacted on his work in verse: there is clear evidence of this in the two large poetic compositions which Hrabal wrote at the time and with which his career as a poet peaked: the long Prague poem *Bambino di Praga* (1950) and the long Kladno poem *Poldi, the Beautiful Steelworks* (1951).

---

18) 'Dům, který se osvěžoval bleskem,' in *SSBH,* Vol. 2, pp. 45–46 (trans. DS).

The lyrical framework of both poems (signalled formally by their being in free verse) admittedly allowed a return to a lyrical *Ich*, which is again the sole line along which the statement evolves, but what it is about is, this time, markedly action-focussed, full of latent or indeed explicit story-telling. That which, in *Bambino di Praga*, unites the abrupt confrontations of these brutal and beautiful fragments of storyline (tinged with both the eroticism of the city and a yearning for purity) may, again, be the subject as it activates the fluid principle of Apollinairean association; however, Apollinairean simultaneity is now no longer a mere, casually playful principle of composition, but is promoted to being the poem's actual subject, in consequence of which it, too, is now in the service of new, mimetic intentions. Beneath a bleak nocturne of Prague, full of gross and violent scenes, ancient images emerge from the depths of history, making this urban expressionism the antithesis of the idyll of provincial Nymburk, "life and death / are identical press studs / by Koh-i-noor Waldes",[19] and in the tradition of Apollinaire and Cendrars the identity of the speaker multiplies symptomatically:

But I'm not the coachman, I'm just looking,
nor the idiot Thume, who came and sat opposite me
and shouted: You're a baker!
that was so spot-on that I said: Forsooth I am,
and we played cards all night,
or in the synagogue, where winding its way up to heaven
goes the vine of the cantor's voice
and the Lord pisses down on the prayer shawls,
where the rabbi with the cantor on his back
rides a tightrope and
together they set off fireworks,
there I was approached by a shiny Jew
who whispered: Excuse me, are you also from the East?
While I did reply: No, it's just the way I look,
I then shot off home at full pelt

19) "život a smrt / jsou identické patentky / Koh-i-noor Waldes", 'Zpěv' [Song] in *SSBH*, Vol. 2, pp. 148-173 (169). This is by no means the only occasion when Hrabal uses the press-stud image.

and doused myself at once in the mirror
and read over my birth certificate and proof of domicile... [20]

The vivid segments of reality in *Poldi the Beautiful Steelworks* are recorded with even greater definition, to the extent that in this poem we also see, with an eloquence bordering on the documentary (against the background of an emotional evocation of the steelworks as "an imprint of copper and a singed lock of hair from the stars"), the brutalisation of life in the early 1950s (an image of female prisoners in a labour camp, or of the police persecuting Christian activists). The steelworks is, first and foremost, an intermediate space in which we see manifested the fundamental anarchy of existence, the dynamics and reversibility of its internal oppositions: beauty and ugliness, cruelty and tenderness, life and death.

But this is life and a machine has to keep going,
progress devours roasted young men
and a silver ambulance waits in suspense,
a crushed hand so longs to return
and reverse into the shape it once owned,
so much do lost contents love forms
and vice versa (...)
... it's always some trusting young volunteer
who misgrabs a burning wire with his tongs,
misturns the thirsty steel
and flies in a beautiful ten-metre red arc
into the black air,
and when a loop lands on his neck,
it makes the young volunteer
do a dance
for the benefit of his mates on the line,
variations on the Gruppo del Laocoonte,
oder über die Grenze der Malerei,
where maximum creative pain
seeks a minimally abbreviated touch...[21]

20) Ibid., p. 159 (trans. DS).
21) 'Zpěv' (Song), *Krásná Poldi*, in *SSBH*, Vol. 2, pp. 194–224 (197–198) (trans. DS).

The associative principle operates here on both the semantic plane (assemblages of images as signs of the prolific chaos of life), and on the plane of poetic syntax. However, the juxtaposition of images is even more radical than in *Bambino di Praga*, and the original Apollinairean simultaneity is replaced by the related, though not coincident method of collage. This shift is, once again, a step back from the lyrical *Ich* (as the element steering the process of association, organising it and consolidating it all-inclusively) towards the prosaic tacking-on of additional segments, whose perspective is still not unequivocally determined by the organising subject and opens the work up to unregulated interpretation by the reader. Thus, here too, Hrabal is, within the poem's space, building up his poetics of "total realism", which seeks to be as impersonal and iconic as possible. Within the logic of this, the text also has long passages of reproduced speech, "things people say", worked into it, served up in the warts-an'-all authenticity of prefabricated, ready-made, nuggets:

An' if she won't fit in 't coffin?
We'll break 't old biddy's legs!
Okay,
in forty-eight soles cost
seventy crowns
and today, cos everything's got so much better,
only a hundred an' sixty!
Since the time they got burgled
they've loved each other.
Have they been trying to mark you one down, waiter?
I'm one mark up, and no one can take that from me![22]

22) Ibid., p. 201 (trans. DS).

IV

Both methods – collage and the impersonally recorded utterance – were not surfacing in these two long narrative poems for the first time: they found their way into them as techniques that had been tried and tested, if only recently: Hrabal had tried out the unamended record of a stream of speech in *The Sorrows of Old Werther* and put collage to the test in *Mrtvomat* (title not usually translated or translatable, unless perhaps as 'Mortumat';[23] both texts date from 1949).

With *The Sorrows of Old Werther* Hrabal's "literary destiny" was invaded for the first time by Uncle Pepin (his stepfather's brother, Josef Hrabal, 1882–1967). Uncle Pepin, portraits of whom were to recur in Hrabal's later works, was an extrovert oddball brimming with vitality, whose pathological loquacity had fascinated Hrabal ever since his childhood in Nymburk. Whenever Pepin spoke, all sorts of things came out, higgledy-piggledy, with absolutely no sense of hierarchy; they included cock-and-bull stories, funny sketches, snatches of dialogue, quotations from everywhere and nowhere, notions conveyed by cliché alone, all swept into the homogeneous stream of his inarticulate discourse by some unfathomable, parasurrealistic associative mechanism. *The Sorrows of Old Werther* came about as an "official record" of his uncle's yarn-spinning, typed up by Hrabal in seven instalments from his uncle's visits to Prague.

> So we wrote these records seven times in total, I even started to enjoy the stream of sentences, stories I'd heard told so many times before at home or in company on the banks of the Elbe, at the neighbours', but like a true Chasid I showed my surprise and feigned an astonishment that just fed the embers of the source of the storytelling, I even kept my uncle supplied with beer so he would keep talking on and on until fatigue overcame him, and it was only with the act of writing that I saw that these topsy-turvy tales did, after all, have an order of their own, I would be quite on edge in advance in case Uncle Pepin lost track of where he'd broken off... and indeed, after several minutes, following other stories that, out of the blue, he'd felt impelled to tell, he'd be back,

23) 'Mrtvomat' is actually a jocular folk designation for a funeral parlour, cf. 'laundromat'. [DS]

picking up where almost two pages before he had stopped, and on he talked, letting himself get swept along by the urgency of an image that rose before him like an atomic mushroom so that he had to finish that which had magically loomed back, and sometimes a given image would undergo its own fission and start exploding into ever more images like a firework display.[24]

The text in question, having come into being the way it had, was fundamental to Hrabal's further development. Its place among his other texts of the time is obviously exceptional and its status as literature distinctly wobbly. Jankovič hits the nail on the head describing this "official record" as by nature "pre-literary": "Pepin's illogicality takes us back to the authentic seeing and experiencing of reality *before* literature."[25] It is an experiment: what is being sought is a point of contact between the oral and the literary. For this mode of presentation to have "become possible" (Jankovič), Hrabal was to have to amend, condense and rationalise it in *Taneční hodiny pro starší a pokročilé* (Dancing Lessons for the Advanced in Age).[26] However, it remains undeniable that it was this most peculiar authorial collaboration with a crazy folk rhapsodist that enabled Hrabal to put his finger on the vital core of primal, naïve storytelling, and to access a narrative energy as yet unenfeebled and unregulated by bookish stylisation – what he was later to call *pábení* (variously translated as 'palavering' or 'rambling on').[27] Uncle Pepin revealed to an astonished Hrabal the most fundamental mechanisms by which life can metamorphose into words. Taking a lesson from the experience, Hrabal's later short stories would be filled with people talking, he being the recorder of the things they say: the characters who take to the stage in his writings in prose will not be psychological movers of plots, but – as had once happened before, in the *Tales from a Thousand and One Nights* – "character-narratives".[28]

---

24) Note 2.9 on *Utrpení starého Werthera* in 'Poznámky, Různočtení, Varianty' [Notes, Divergences, Variants], *SSBH*, Vol. 2, pp. 239–244 (240).

25) Jankovič, Milan: *Kapitoly z poetiky Bohumila Hrabala*, Prague: Torst, 1996, p. 34.

26) For an English translation of this work see the Appendix. [DS]

27) But which for present purposes I shall translate as "yarn-spinning". [DS]

28) In the sense introduced by Tzvetan Todorov; see his *Poétique de la prose*, Paris: Seuil, 1978 (first published 1971), p. 37: "Tout récit [*Les Mille et une nuits*] ne consiste

However, Uncle Pepin had yet another impact on Hrabal's work: through the prism of Pepin's stories, Hrabal could harness to his own prose images of old Austria-Hungary, richly tinted in the manner of Hašek's humoresques. It is strikingly symptomatic of the poetics of Hrabal the "recorder" that this stratum invades his prose in the same casual manner as the era of the First Republic, the wartime Protectorate or the later age of communism: in Hrabal's evocation of the times of the Habsburg monarchy there is no historicising; quite the contrary: he makes it look as if this, too, is just another part of his personal postmortemising.

How the *Mrtvomat* collage came into being was described by Hrabal himself: the core layer is an overheard conversation between two poets, Jiří Kolář and Kamil Bednář, concerning the sale and purchase of puppets ("I say, Kolář, have you got another death?"); to this are attached in studied configurations – arranged almost *à la* Mallarmé – lists of toys drawn from a maker's invoice, inscriptions from headstones in the cemetery at Nymburk, a price list from a spa, a leaflet from the *Krematorium* society, notes on the instructions given by a traffic policeman and a report from what the Czechs call the 'black chronicle' – the section of a newspaper given over to the most gruesome murders, accidents and the like. In terms of technique and method, the crazy, yet precise way in which the whole has been selected and arranged is the polar opposite of the undoctored record of Uncle Pepin's endless ramblings, yet the reader experience of each is remarkably similar: in both cases the reader is assailed by massive doses of raw chunks of a specific reality. The words with which Hrabal accompanied *Mrtvomat* summarise in a uniquely precise manner the basic components of the poetics at which he had arrived (including the existential reasons that motivated it):

Despair and desolation had gripped my [...] throat [...] My sole recourse was for me to evict myself from myself and board up my heart like a suspect well. I wasn't even minded to oppose the absurdity of the age with the absurdity of my own self. And so I became a pile of bills, inscriptions, a warehouse for furniture and wardrobes. Anything except

pas en une «description de caractères» [...] Tout nouveau personnage signifie une nouvelle intrigue. Nous sommes dans le royaume des hommes-récits."

me myself [...] A window had been knocked into my self, and so also from my self out. I was no longer alone! Dozens of things of which I had no inkling shared my lot and were all lucky enough to be unable to complain. And I stiffened my fibre and felt ashamed of my question marks and exclamation marks and interjections. Even in this day and age one has had to be hard and anonymous, like an invoice from TOFA,[29] like a stone. The fallen leaves of my sentimentality covered everything, so I could see nothing. And at that moment I did see that everything had its own order and beauty. You just needed to become it. To know how to bash yourself into things. [...] You just have to mark well that reality is true, holy craziness.[30]

Thus in the *Mrtvomat* collage Hrabal's quest for the impersonality and iconicity of "total realism" reached its peak: his "recorder" mode is here taken to extremes. This quite distinctive type of collage might have resurfaced only one more time in Hrabal's work (in the textual accompaniment to Miroslav Peterka's photographs of Prague entitled *toto město je ve společné péči obyvatel* [this city is in the joint care of its inhabitants[31]], 1967),[32] but as a compositional principle it had earned its keep. Incidentally, the way Hrabal uses collage serves to remind us just how important the graphic arts generally were to the shaping of his poetics. And last but not least: *Mrtvomat* again reminds us of the interpenetration of the lyrical and narrational principles in Hrabal's work: it may also be read, quite legitimately, as a Cubist-Surrealist poem.

---

29) A former large Czech(oslovak) toymaking company; the name is an acronym from Toy Factory. [DS]

30) 'Expozé', *Mrtvomat*, in *SSBH*, Vol. 2, pp. 141-143 (trans. DS).

31) The absence of capitalisation of the first word is entirely deliberate. For a fairly detailed, illustrated, study of this unusual work see David Short: 'Fun and Games with Montage: the Individual Case of Hrabal's *toto město je ve společné péči obyvatel*' in Short: *Bohumil Hrabal*, pp. 59–81. [DS]

32) It was reworked and included under the title *Legenda zahraná na strunách napjatých mezi legendou a rakví* [A legend played on strings stretched between legend and coffin] in *Morytáty a legendy* [Gory-stories and legends).

V

The turbulent period of 1949–52, when Hrabal's poetics was taking shape, saw, besides the two poetic highlights that are *Bambino di Praga* and *Poldi the Beautiful Steelworks*, the birth of two extraordinarily mature works in prose: at the start (1949) came the "existentialist short story" 'Cain' (reworked in 1965 into the novella *Ostře sledované vlaky* [Closely Watched Trains[33]] and included in 1968, in a form close to the original and under the title *Legenda o Kainovi* [The Legend of Cain], in the collection *Morytáty a legendy* [Gory-stories and Legends]), and at the end the short story *Jarmilka* (1952), published, in a self-censored form, in the collection *Pábitelé* (Palaverers,[34] 1964) and, slightly modified, under the title *Majitelka hutí* (The Owner of the Ironworks – with more than a nod to Georges Ohnet's *Le Maître de forges*), in *Flower Buds* (1970). Both works are also characteristic products of Hrabal's grand season of experimentation: yet again they are attempts, quite unlike each other, to find a personal narrative syntax. But they are also experiments not limited to just exploring certain options, given that they also implement those options in an utterly unique manner.

When *Closely Watched Trains* came out in the mid-1960s, it was greeted – as against its broadly positive reception – by critical opposition from the pen of Jan Lopatka. Lopatka seems to have been caught off-guard by the fact that Hrabal, who had already found his niche on the literary stage with prose that dispensed with *syuzhet* and instead bombarded the reader with "a string of motifs, any one of which lent itself to independent development",[35] had created in *Closely Watched Trains* a text that was slotted into a particular genre

---

33) Other translated versions of this title also exist, *viz Closely Observed Trains* and (the earliest) *A Close Watch on the Trains*, all heading a common translation by Edith Pargeter (see appendix). 'Closely watched' is the version used for the eponymous film. [DS]

34) I accept this more or less established translation for *pábitel* with misgivings; I have avoided it in other contexts wherever possible, usually referring in English to such individuals as 'yarn-spinners'; cf. the volume *Rambling On...* (see checklist in Appendix). [DS]

35) Lopatka, Jan: *Předpoklady tvorby. Výběr kritických článků a recenzí z let 1965–1969*, Prague: Československý spisovatel, 1991, p. 14.

paradigm (it "put content into an appropriated structure") and told a story that was, up to a point, its author's commentary on history. Lopatka believed that Hrabal had sold out to "the ethics of creativity" and taken the path of "writerhood", meaning that he had adopted the way of writing in which "motifs, scenes and characters cease to exist and become constructed bearers of meaning".[36]

Whether or not we share Lopatka's high expectations of literature, there is no doubting that he put his finger on the crux of the matter: within the totality of Hrabal's oeuvre, *Closely Watched Trains* is a quite isolated attempt at constructing a plot, both the plot and the characters on which it rests having a more general symbolic reach. Yet this is also true of the source text, the short story 'Cain', and Lopatka might well have shown greater indulgence had he been in a position to take this genetic link into consideration. With 'Cain' Hrabal had attempted to write an "existentialist short story" (as we read beneath the work's title): by how the *syuzhet* is construed – as a story of an "Everyman" – he had sought to symbolise the basic factors that determine human existence. The goal is realised with amazing concision, unburdened by any extraneous motifs (at this stage the subject of resistance is not developed, nor is there an anti-hero condemned to unpremeditated heroism). The text's intensity is enormous: it comes as no surprise to read in the postscript, which Hrabal added in 1981, the admission that he had felt impelled to write it, "as if in a dark cloud", and that whenever he re-read the text later, he found it quite spine-chilling. We know from Hrabal's own testimony that, in addition to the autobiographical motifs, three literary texts on love and death are projected into the text: Goethe's *The Sorrows of Young Werther*, Dante's *Vita Nuova* and Camus' *L'Étranger*.

Hrabal undoubtedly read Camus aright, his protagonist evincing the same willingness to accept the absurdity of his existence as Camus' Meursault:

> I was always submissive, because it was safer, because I believed in a fate which, whenever the fancy took it, would arm me with a will, only to break my back with it in the very next instant.[37]

36) Ibid., p. 15.
37) 'Kain', in *SSBH*, Vol. 2, pp. 7–37 (11). (Hereafter 'Kain', trans. DS).

I always did honestly what it had just befallen me to do.[38]

At the start of the work the hero attempts none the less to commit suicide: by this willed death he wants defiantly to wrest his freedom from God.[39]

One day God will pray to this victorious man, because He will be superfluous.[40]

But freedom is denied him: he is saved and re-awakens to life, moreover as someone who has crossed the frontier of darkness, who is no longer the person he was, and who cannot recognise himself in the mirror.

The blood pumped in at top prices made me into someone else, someone cautious, fearful, literary. [...] My forehead was horror-spattered at the sight of myself, but I went, because I was honest and always did whatever dangled before me.[41]

Instead of death desired, life undesired is back. After returning to this life – with the mark of Cain on his wrist – the hero finds that his girlfriend is pregnant. The world is about to be blessed with yet another unwanted life and the man's story will be retold in the story of his child.

I suddenly knew that nothing had been terminated, that death can solve nothing, postpone nothing. Even if I had killed myself in Bystřice four months back, life would have gone on. So it would have been good for them to have saved me, because the child about to be born to me will need protection. It will not and cannot be anything different from me

38) Ibid., p. 13
39) The motif of rebellion against God – surely inspired more by Ladislav Klíma than Camus – is to be found elsewhere in the early Hrabal, notably in the remarkable prose poem 'Slavná Wantochova legenda' (The glorious legend of Wantoch) from the *Menorah* collection, written in the tradition of carnival culture and baroque *danses macabres*.
40) 'Kain', p. 19.
41) Ibid., p. 22.

and my forebears. So it will need someone capable of explaining to it who it's down to, it will be necessary to apologise to it for its having been brought into the world. I knew that the child would be born with an invisible scar on its wrist, because the beginnings of the wound will be in its soul.[42]

At the story's end, with the war just over and transports of German POWs moving through the district, the hero dies: having helped a fatally wounded German soldier to die, he is himself hit by a stray bullet. He dies an unwanted death: that real, fatal, cruel and unjust death that sends man back to the beginning.

> I knew that it was the end of me and that I had to remain in the pain which I had neither wished for nor caused. I was lying in a ditch with a scarf of blood, and with every stirring of the breeze petals of plum blossom showered down on me. [...] In a single flash or, rather, through the crack in a door that had banged shut, I had a vision of my suicide, and it was such a dear, sweet thing. All the other deaths were brutish and unjust. [...] I kicked my legs like a child in a tantrum and the world vanished.[43]

The importance of this text goes beyond its contiguity with Camus' existentialism and the evidence that it therefore furnishes of how Hrabal's post-war output was in synchrony with what was happening in literature elsewhere in Europe. It is important in its own right: for the way it is pitched in terms of stylisation (Hrabal's "eidetic memory", fascinated by detail, is crossed with the hypersensitive factuality of Camus' narrative style), then as an experiment in symbolic construction of a narrative, but above all as evidence of Hrabal's keen interest in interpreting the world philosophically. The point here being that just one among the many paradoxes about Hrabal's writing is precisely the oscillation between his poignant acceptance of existence in the infinitude of its manifestations, i.e. what he himself was later to call his "undiscriminating observation", a term borrowed from the verse of Viola Fischerová, in an extract

42) Ibid., p. 33.
43) Ibid., pp. 36–37.

placed after the title page of *Inzerát na dům, ve kterém už nechci bydlet* (A For-sale Ad for a House in Which I No Longer Wish to Live),[44] and the constantly surfacing need to find a metaphysical explanation for it. This version of "existentialism" was also apparent in the previously mentioned short story 'The House that was Refreshed by Lightning', and shades of it were to come back in numerous future works, but particularly momentously in *Too Loud a Solitude*. It seems fair to generalise and say that Hrabal's future texts dominated by storytelling will be typified by the principle of "undiscriminating observation", while whenever he evinces that lyrical hankering after "begetting in the beautiful", that urge will be underpinned by a clear metaphysical perspective.

The lyrical segments of *Jarmilka* also have a metaphysical ring, though this time merely as one angle of vision, perhaps more profound and essential than others, but often in competition with, and frequently overlaid by them. This work, too, has a story line (and again concerns the birth of a child), and it is also not quite free of a symbolic overhang: at the metaphorical level it can still be read as an exemplum *sui generis*. As an exemplum, however, it is nowhere near as atemporal as 'Cain', being, on the contrary, very much of its time and the most incisive literary image of the 1950s ever written in Czech. But then the main story is entwined by runners from the many other stories derived from the other characters who come into play (*hommes-récits*[45]). *Jarmilka* (whose subtitle identifies it in genre terms as a "documentary", thereby hinting at the poetics of "total realism") is a kind of distillation of Hrabal's years of experimentation, a kind of *Gesamtkunstwerk* in which he achieved a unique amalgam of all the methods that he had so far put to the test: collage, the impersonality that "bashes itself into things", records of streams of speech, the lyrical confrontation of brutality and tenderness, and an undercurrent of profound existential reflection.

It is this complex orchestration of narrative devices that gives *Jarmilka* its uniquely liberated character: we are happy to forget that it is underpinned by the huge effort put into its construction, given that it is anything but a mere addition of content to an "appropri-

44) *SSBH*, Vol. 5, p. 116.
45) See Note 28.

ated structure". It is not a story that imitates life, but – to borrow the happy formulation applied by Vladislav Vančura to Josef Štefan Kubín – "the current of life fashioned into a story".[46] In the centre of the narrative construct is the figure of Jarmilka, a simple proletarian lass from the ranks of the "insulted and humiliated", who is going through her particular, trifling, personal drama, an unexpected pregnancy, but is doing so all the way up the scale from despair to high hope. In a unique manner, Hrabal immerses one banal, personal motif into the vast social cauldron that is the Kladno steelworks: this individual destiny is played out on the set of the hugely complex *theatrum mundi* of the 1950s, among a host of extras represented by workers, female convicts and intellectuals drafted into production, and maladjusted gypsies. These extras have, of course, each their own story, sometimes quite remarkable, for instance the horror story of a concentration camp inmate and die-hard communist, named Hannes by Hrabal after his friend of the time, the painter Hanes Reegen, or the "legends" of the new Soviet Russia vividly delivered by the shock-worker Mudra. The words used by the steelworks – and by Jarmilka – are often coarse, vulgar, yet they are tellingly exact, full of evocative power, and they ring out with all the more force for being heard against the background of the banalities uttered by the "loudspeaker bullshitters" who debase reality to an ideologically motivated utopia. This world is not judged, but empathised with: it is at once dreadful and beautiful, tragic and comic (its comic aspects illuminated by a humour rooted in Pirandello-esque *sentimento del contrario*), "fantastic and realistic".[47] It is depicted by means of a continuous counterpoint between high and low, the small-scale and the grand-scale: Jarmilka's heroic journey in search of an unassuming happiness is never once overlaid by the tragedy of the age. And then, through the chinks between the individual "things said" by this or that character, its lyrical hypostasis springs to the surface.

Hrabal's prose is naturally and fundamentally at variance with the tawdry optimism of the slogans that went with the building of socialism; for him, life is no easy or joyful matter, and here, too,

---

46) Vladislav Vančura: 'J. Š. Kubín', in: Idem, *Řád nové tvorby,* eds. Milan Blahynka and Štěpán Vlašín. Prague: Svoboda 1972, p. 448.
47) *Jarmilka*, in *SSBH*, Vol. 3, pp. 88–125 (102), (trans. DS).

in *Jarmilka*, he is conveying the existential malaise of the Meursault-like Cain: one must

> resign oneself to automatism, cherished and rigorous especially first thing in the morning, by when not to live has become impossible.[48]

And yet, this attitude is not resignation, but re-acceptance:

> I'm standing above the women convicts and seeing that life doesn't end anywhere, and that the very point at which it wouldn't be expected is where it begins.[49]

It is precisely from the standpoint of this existential malaise that Hrabal proved able, in this work, to express the pathos of workplace collectivism with a credibility denied to all the period prose works given over to the construction of socialism:

> Being sort of buckled together by labour is a platform on which we can brush against one another, while otherwise we are beyond one another's grasp.[50]

48) Ibid., p. 123.
49) Ibid., p. 91.
50) Ibid., p. 124.

VI

Jarmilka was Hrabal's only prosework from his early years post-apprenticeship of which he repeatedly regretted that it had not been published at the time of writing. This tells us that he was himself fully aware that in it he had reached the final formulation of a poetics that owed nothing to anyone and fitted his talent to perfection. Be it recalled that Hrabal had the knack of always appraising his own texts with precision, and that the best reviews of them generally came from his own pen in occasional self-assessments. The poetics of *Jarmilka* duly returns in most of the things that were to accumulate in his bottom drawer during the decade that followed and some of which began to appear in print from the start of the 1960s. As mentioned previously, Hrabal first went public (if we ignore the 1956 bibliophile print of *Things People Say*) with the short-story collection *Pearls of the Deep* in 1963; one previous attempt at a selection of his stories, under the title *Skřivánek na niti* (Skylark on a Thread) and prepared by the Československý spisovatel publishing house for 1959, was blocked by the censor and the already set type was broken up. Then following *Pearls* in rapid succession came *Palaverers* (1964), *Dancing Lessons for the Advanced in Age* (1964), *Closely Watched Trains* (1965), *A For-sale Ad for a House in Which I No Longer Wish to Live* (1965) and *Gory-stories and Legends* (1968).

For the most part, all these texts were a gradual opening-up – if largely in reworked versions and textual "variations" – of the earliest stratum of Hrabal's post-war output, and while on the face of it they looked, in the more relaxed atmosphere of the 1960s, like a unique outburst of creativity, for Hrabal himself (whose 1963 debut came a year before his fiftieth birthday) they meant a concentrated stocktaking of the path he had already trodden. The systematic nature of this process, whereby each publication went a further step backwards to successively earlier works, was sealed by the last volume in the sequence, the oft-mentioned *Flower Buds* (*Poupata*) of 1970, in which Hrabal had decided to give access to the earliest of all his manuscripts, including his early works in verse. However, this collection, printed after the Soviet invasion of Czechoslovakia and in the atmosphere of incipient hardline "normalisation", shared the fate of *Skylark on a Thread* and most of the print run ended up being pulped.

If the poetics of Hrabal's texts as they built up over the 1950s was fairly uniform, this does not mean that it was completely without change or that the accent on this or that aspect did not shift somewhat. The time for grand experimentation might have passed, but even within a stabilised poetics there was still room for its limits to be continually tested and for the range of subjects to be expanded. Hrabal the recorder came into contact with more and more new environments, which he automatically drew into the magic circle of his poetic vision: he allowed particular voices to come out of these environments and used his collage method to set various things they said against each other.

One constant, conspicuous thematic element of the entire "hypertext" of the 1950s and 1960s is Hrabal's background in the small town of Nymburk. In 'Lednová povídka' (January Story) and 'Únorová povídka' (February Story) (written in 1952 and published in *Flower Buds*) we find another portrait of Uncle Pepin, though not this time in the mirror of his monologue (as in *The Sorrows of Old Werther* and *Dancing Lessons for the Advanced in Age*), but (in line with the poetics of *Jarmilka*) as a unique human type whose utterances this time represent the stones in the narrative mosaic, completely under the author's direction. Hrabal's stepfather Francin is also evoked with affection as an enthusiastic pioneer of motoring ('Večerní kurs' [Evening course] in *Pearls of the Deep*) and, marginally, even his mother ('Smrt pana Baltisbergera' [The Death of Mr Baltisberger], *ibid.*); however, the family story only comes to dominate Hrabal's prose rather later, in the 1970s. In the exquisite short story 'Jeden všední den' (One Ordinary Day, written in 1952, first published in 1987 in the volume *Atomová mašina Perkeo* [The Perkeo Atomic Typewriter]) Hrabal also brings in his friend from Nymburk, the poet Karel Marysko (he will resurface in 'Chcete vidět zlatou Prahu' [Want to See Golden Prague?] in *Palaverers*). In a heroi-comic scene where Marysko learns that Prof. Václav Černý, a major figure in Czech literary history and criticism, had had his house searched by the police – and he and Hrabal had both entrusted manuscripts to Černý – we are again afforded a sightline into the anxious atmosphere of the 1950s. At the same time, there is an unconscious reflection of the shift in Hrabal's poetics away from the times of his "Art nouveau tinkerings in verse":

> They'll ask you: Did you write this? And if you say: No, then smash, one straight in the gob, and again: Did you write it? Smash, an' another in the gob. And finally they'll ask: Did you write it? And you'll say: Yeah. So they'll hit you again for having lied, and you'll have a cloud in your trousers. Oh, if only I was brave, but I'm scared, that's the thing, I'm scared, everybody's scared…. […] Take your gothic man, he was used to it, torture barely bothered him, but I'm completely done for by the very idea of it… shallow land of mine with your fine lacework of ramparts, wagging a tower like a finger at the far distance… why on earth didn't we have the sense to stay in Nymburk and not start writing crap like that?[51]

Hrabal's prose gradually fills up ever more strikingly with people from the highly picturesque milieus that he came to know through his bizarre employment history: railwaymen (in 'Fádní stanice' [Lacklustre Station] and then in *Closely Watched Trains*) and insurance agents ('Andělský voči' [Angel Eyes] in *Pearls of the Deep*, 'Bambini di Praga 1947' in *Palaverers*), are followed into Hrabal's writings by the personnel at a paper-recycling centre ('Baron Prášil' [Baron Munchhausen] in *Pearls of the Deep*, where we first meet Haňťa, the future protagonist of *Too Loud a Solitude*), and stagehands ('Pražské jesličky' [A Prague Nativity], also in *Pearls of the Deep*). Pride of place among these environments goes to the steelworks at Kladno ('Miláček' [Darling] in *Pearls of the Deep* and above all three supreme evocations of the Stalinist period: 'Divní lidé' [Strange People], 'Anděl' [Angel] and 'Ingot a ingoti' [Ingot and Ingots[52]] in *A For-sale Ad for a House in Which I No Longer Wish to Live*).

Hrabal describes these environments from the inside: he maps them out with precision through the prism of what people say, giving the floor to people whose entire lives have been fused with their milieu, who therefore speak of it in the most apposite language, in

---

51) 'Jeden všední den', in *SSBH*, Vol. 3, pp. 200–211 (207) (trans. DS).

52) It is not obvious in translation that the word *Ingoti* is marked grammatically for animacy, i.e. refers to humans. For a broader and deeper analysis of what Hrabal was doing by this simple device see Zuzana Stolz-Hladká: 'Bohumil Hrabal and the Corporality of the Word', in Short: *Bohumil Hrabal*, pp. 35–49 (36–37, 39). [DS]

words that fit the given environment to perfection. The discourse of these speakers is consequently highly concrete: it literally touches the objects about them, giving rise to quite original turns of phrase that capture the finer details brought out in this unusually sharp lighting; and it abounds in the slang terminology that makes life so hard for Hrabal's translators. In terms of the history of literature, this amounts, among other things, to a return to the Naturalist poetics of the second half on the nineteenth century that sought so single-mindedly to purvey almost photographic descriptions of specific milieus. However, there is still a considerable difference between how the Naturalists and Hrabal see things: it is not Hrabal's intention to furnish an objective account of these environments: he is merely presenting them through the experience of those who are immersed in them and make them what they are. Images of these environments are lit up by a sympathy that is open-eyed and willing to exaggerate and magnify. The language of the characters here is, thus, not merely a means to evoke a reality, but the actual living voice of these spheres of existence. We almost always see these environments – as previously in *Jarmilka* – when they are busy: language looms over specific tasks at hand and work is, again, the "clasp" that holds individual solitudes together and lets separate stories flow into the polyphony of a conversation that is constantly having bits tacked onto it.

One conspicuous feature of these environments is how much they are "of the common people". Hrabal has a profound respect for ordinary folk and their faculty for amazement, laughter and grappling with reality. Furthermore, Hrabal is unusual as one of the tiny minority of Czech writers who – beyond the parameters of sociological documentation, so by pure empathy – have drawn unusually sensitive pictures of the Gypsy community (first in *Jarmilka*, then in 'Romance' in *Palaverers*). Quite early on he developed his greatest fondness for Libeň, a typical part of Prague's proletarian periphery, where he settled in 1950.

He drew it as a never-ending "movable feast", full of odd little people perfectly in tune with their everyday existence and beguiled, with no hint of revolt or dissent, both by its mundane splendour and its cut-throat brutality – like a microcosm with a unique atmosphere living out its turbulent life surrounded by banality and far removed from "big history" ('Fádní odpoledne' [A Dull Afternoon], 'Emánek' [Little Eman] and 'Pražské jesličky' [A Prague Nativity] from *Pearls of the Deep*, and 'Pohřeb' [The Funeral], 'Automat Svět' [The World Cafeteria], 'Dáma s kaméliemi' [The Lady of the Camellias] and 'Romance' in *Palaverers*). This typical focus in Hrabal's prose of the period on the "little" people who do not make history is further evidence of the European dimension of his *Tendenz*: while being "apolitical", he is actually being hugely "political", his work calling into question the recent "engaged" literature that sought actively to lend history a hand as it changed the points (in the wider European context, an example of a writer who comes close to Hrabal in this regard is Raymond Queneau). It is no coincidence that this was the time when Hrabal became friends with some of the members of Group 42 (the poet Jiří Kolář, the graphic designer Kamil Lhoták), a group that likewise, by focussing on the everyday life of ordinary people and on the poetics of the marginal, sought a new, ethically unproblematised authenticity of discourse.

Hrabal, enchanted though he was by the vitality of the under-class, was of course an intellectual who circulated among intellectu-als. So in due time they also win his attention: the short stories 'Ex-ploze Gabriel' (The Gabriel Explosion), 'Made in Czechoslovakia' and 'Blitzkrieg' (presumably written in 1952, but reworked and included under the single title 'Legenda o Egonu Bondym a Vladimírkovi' [The Legend of Egon Bondy and Young Vladimír] in *Gory-stories and Legends*) portray his two closest friends at the beginning of the 1950s: the prosewriter and philosopher Egon Bondy (real name Zbyněk Fišer) and the artist Vladimír Boudník; he was to return to both of them in the lyrical memoir *Něžný barbar* (Tender Barbarian), written in 1973. Their presence in these earlier texts is in no sense the intrusion of an alien element: they were both, like Hrabal him-self at the time, outsiders, and, like the plebeian figures of Libeň, could claim a place only at the very fringes of history. Boudník's work won recognition only several decades later (largely thanks to Hrabal's writings about him), while Bondy's prose and verse of the 1950s only emerged from deep underground in the 1990s. Their work, like Hrabal's, was driven by their interest in the fantastic potential lurking in the most intimate and most mundane: Boudník forged a trend that he called "explosionalism" and taught random passers-by to see, in the stains on old walls, works of art, while Bondy's ditties registered the banality of the everyday in a spirit of naïviste, elementary "total realism". This humility in the face of reality and their enduring capacity for amazement are also what tie their literary incarnations most visibly to Hrabal's yarn-spinners among the common folk:

> Vladimír drew my attention to the monument: A mad woman was climbing up it... first onto Huss's finger, then up onto his head.... The fire brigade came... oh how sad and glorious it was... over there on that wall... no, there!, I drew the wall and people really did think they were badly damaged frescoes... they saw what I'd hinted at in those patches...[53]

> A tram was heading off along the embankment and Bondy says: "Look sharp, Doctor, over yonder it looks as if a tram is heading off along the embankment."[54]

In Hrabal's writings, this sense of astonishment (again of a conspicuously lyrical quality) illuminates everything that a narrator's words sieze upon. It constantly adds value to the things to which it attaches itself. In these texts Hrabal lets others speak – without amending, contextualising or passing comment on what they say – and this manner leaves unspoken his basic unwillingness to catalogue facts or place them in any kind of hierarchy or any unequivocally moral perspective. We can surely see in his choice of this approach yet another response to the collectively binding moralising of the official literature of the Stalinist era, and yet his motives are undoubtedly much more subjective and autonomous and much less determined by the period context than might seem at first sight: it is a product of the conviction that Hrabal advanced in the postscript to *Mrtvomat*, namely that we can only "bash ourselves" into things (and people) by accepting their truth, without being selective in principle and without adopting a particular angle in advance; and once again we are reminded that this principle of inventorisation without

---

53) 'Exploze Gabriel', in *SSBH*, Vol. 3, pp. 70-77 (73) (trans. DS).
54) 'Legenda o Egonu Bondym a Vladimírkovi', in *SSBH*, Vol. 5, pp. 246-60 (246) (trans DS).

prior interpretation went with the times: it is also propounded by the *nouveau roman* of Robbe-Grillet, notwithstanding the obvious disparity between these two applications of the principle in literature. Hrabal's "amoralism" was genuinely perceived as polemicising with literary *bienséance* as codified by the aesthetics of the period. Of that there can be no doubt: he himself testified ironically to the fact in the preamble to *Gory-stories and Legends*, where he cited, in parallel, both upbeat and definitely downbeat responses from his readers:

> You foul-mouthed pig, who everybody's praising to the high heavens, when are you going to stop poisoning people's souls with your disgusting perversions?[55]

There can be no doubting that Hrabal's "recorder" poetics directly implies this kind of "a-morality". However, despite being a seemingly marginal problem, it does merit closer attention, being directly relevant to the role of the "narrator" as constituted in these texts.

At first sight there is usually no narrator: he has gone off-stage, leaving the floor to others (in some trial texts completely so, as in the story 'Dětský dům' [A Children's Home], where all we have is a male voice intertwined with a female), his role restricted at best to "stage directions".[56] If ever Hrabal does project himself into his writings, then it is only as a character contributing his own part to a dialogue-based collage, in such cases as, say, 'One Ordinary Day', 'Evening Course' or 'The Legend of Egon Bondy and Young Vladimír', or he might put himself in as a witness, as, for example, in *Jarmilka*. It would appear that the narrator Hrabal kept himself hidden so as not to compromise his role as recorder and so not to have to pass judgement.

---

55) 'Morytát, který napsali čtenáři' (A gory-story written by my readers), in *SSBH*, Vol. 5, pp. 241–45 (243) (trans. DS).
56) It is worth mentioning in this connection that many of Hrabal's prose pieces of this period proved highly amenable to film adaptation and helped enhance the renown of the Czech New Wave, represented by such names as Jiří Menzel, Věra Chytilová, Ivan Passer, Evald Schorm, Jan Němec, Juraj Herz and Jaromil Jireš; the texts could often be used as ready-made screenplays.

In the case of Hrabal, this "disappearance" of the narrator's voice has not even the remotest kinship with Flaubertian *impassibilité*: it is manifestly obvious that what our recorder is recording is entirely in his power and that he remains the supreme demiurge (*deus absconditus*) of these images. The configuration of the fragments from which they are assembled is artificial in the extreme, the author's intention being, beyond all doubt, to create not a perfect fiction, a flawless mirror image of reality *à la* Flaubert, but something that, on the contrary, seeks to provoke by means of its abrupt, always surprising and often astounding, cuts, which will not allow us, even for a moment, to lapse into some blind belief in the "truthfulness" of the image and has us constantly questioning our preconception of the world. At the seams where these sudden cuts are made something problematical always surfaces, something that bids the reader adopt a personal, and often ethically motivated, response. Such a response is not actually programmed into the text, but is usually quite obviously triggered afresh. Seeing things in this light, we can appreciate Hrabal's obvious satisfaction when, in the preamble to *Gory-stories*, he copies verbatim the letters of people who berate him as an immoral beast; for him this is proof that his challenge has not gone unheard. The narrator in these texts may be hidden, but in reality no "recorder" can dissolve completely into anonymity; some trace of him will always remain, now more, now less in evidence (in the qualifying adjectives used, in the details highlighted or in the manner in which different segments of the text are tacked onto one another). In *Jarmilka* another such trace is the Dostoyevskyan-Tolstoyan compassion evinced; this will resurface later, and much more explicitly, in, for example, the final chapter of *Obsluhoval jsem anglického krále* (I Waited on the King of England[57]), and, among the even "more impersonal" texts set in Kladno, there is, in *A For-sale Ad for a House in Which I No Longer Wish to Live*, a trace of Céline-esque resigned despair.

Hrabal is certainly no moralist: we would be hard put to it to find anywhere in his work an unambiguously positive hero, or at least an ideal, noble representative of mankind. The one telling

---

57) Habitually mistranslated as 'I Served the King of England', though the latter title, being widely felt as standard, will, therefore, be used hereafter. [DS]

exception is Miloš Hrma in *Closely Watched Trains*, a book which might be respecting a certain convention of the genre, but in which Miloš is actually thrown out of kilter by his own pubertal immaturity. Hrabal is clearly interested more in "problematical" than "pure" characters, and he clearly exhibits a greater interest in "average" than in "above-average" people. But he is never interested in them for any particular pathology, but for how, in terms of the society in which they are immersed, it is possible to discern some feature of value, a feature that is the very point through which this or that person steps outside solitude and egoism and which enables him to live if not *for* others, then at least *with* others ("pearls from the depths" is certainly an ethical metaphor as well). This faculty of Hrabal's characters for breaking out of their solitude – usually by wedging their story into the stories of others – creates that telling atmosphere of sociability that dominates those of his texts that trade on yarn-spinners and ultimately invests many of them with a fragile sense of equilibrium.

Yet these prose texts are far from idyllic, given that the motifs of violence and death are probably more frequent here than in the tragedies of Shakespeare. Of course, the response of the denizens of Hrabal's stories to the profound tragedy of life is usually not their version of sarcasm or irony, but laughter: a matchingly profound, collective, Rabelaisian laughter that does not draw a veil over tragedy, but relativises it and uncovers its ambivalence. Susanne Roth captured the nature of Hrabal's humour to perfection when she identified its supra-personal dimension with a quotation from Karel Čapek: "Humour is a social product... ."[58]

Hrabal's characters, often extremely nebulous as to personal characteristics, usually live solely through their storytelling. Their monologues are, however, no mere faint reflection of life: for them, storytelling is a direct component of life (as for Sheherazade, the archetypal "character-narrative", it is in a sense a matter of life and death). Elsewhere in Europe, perhaps the only person to ascribe a

58) Roth, Susanne: *Laute Einsamkeit und bitteres Glück*. Bern etc.: Peter Lang, 1986, pp. 61–62 (hereafter Roth: *Laute Einsamkeit*). The Čapek quotation is from *Marsyas, čili na okraji literatury* [Marsyas, or: On the fringes of literature], Prague [Spisy Bratří Čapků], 1948, p. 77. It goes on to say that "the best that individualism can rise to is irony".

similarly existential role to human speech is Hrabal's contemporary, Samuel Beckett. For Beckett's heroes, too, having the chance to speak is synonymous with living. The difference between Hrabal and Beckett is – at least at this stage – the difference between the two sides of a coin: in both cases, speaking is in a sense man's final refuge, but, in contrast to Beckett's tragic vision, Hrabal sets human discourse in a euphoric, frolicsome landscape.

The manner of Hrabal's heroes' discourse already attracted the attention of the critics in the 1960s. The main study on the subject was by Emanuel Frynta in 1966:[59] he saw the roots of this never-ending oral performance (something also perceived as uniting Hrabal and Jaroslav Hašek, the progenitor of the Good Soldier Schweik) in the "pub yarn", one typical form of urban folklore. Frynta also provided a near-exhaustive account of the structural features of this folk genre: it is usually part of a broader context (a discussion or party), its subject does not exceed one lifetime and is usually presented as having been experienced personally, it is improvised (though individuals and groups alike may have a constant repertoire of such yarns), and obligatory indicators are the teller's swearing to its truth and his or her fondness for hyperbole. Frynta thus found that the source of Hrabal's rambling narratives lay in that fact of folk, oral performance represented by the intersection between an experience still fresh in the mind and its verbalisation within a particular – however erratic – genre paradigm.

Frynta undoubtedly captured the structural features of this oral artefact precisely, but the very term "pub yarn" simply cannot be taken at face value. It follows from Hrabal's texts that the space where his type of narration is born is not just pubs (and when there's something to celebrate), but also, if not even more so, workplaces and any other situation where people are thrown together naturally. In addition, a pub is a place where, broadly speaking, men do the talking, whereas spinning yarns is not a purely male prerogative, women also playing their yarn-spinning part as if it were the most natural thing in the world. That apart, there is a huge difference between the ways in which the "pub yarn" is used by Hašek and

59) Emanuel Frynta: 'Náčrt základů Hrabalovy prózy', in: Bohumil Hrabal: *Automat Svět. Výbor povídek*. Prague: Mladá fronta, 1966

Hrabal: the yarns put in the mouth of Schweik by Hašek are very often anecdotes that have a point and could even be free-standing, whereas in Hrabal it is a much less clear-cut formation that does something that actually enhances the context into which it is plunged. The reduced autonomy of the pub yarn in Hrabal is a clear signal that it is, for him, merely a basic ingredient that he processes by literary transformation.[60] Roth has correctly observed that this transformation also entails the inclusion of additional material, recalling in this connection Hrabal's predilection for popular, trash literature and for such strictly non-literary artifacts as travel guides, dream-books, anecdotes etc.[61]

The chief instrument of transformation is the unrelenting concatenation of these units, usually on a rising scale. The principle that Hrabal employed most frequently is the series, enumeration, the Rabelaisian endless succession: we are not surprised that this or that happened, but that so very much goes on. Within any such series there is a constant tension, owing to the non-stop, startling clashes between these verbalised fragments of life. In these texts, the fact that no yarn can ever be the last and so has to be picked up by another is emphasised time and again: the inexhaustibility of storytelling is precisely a token of the inexhaustibility of life itself. It is no coincidence that the highpoints of both *Pearls from the Deep* and *Palaverers* are the two longest pieces – constantly extended narrative syntagms: 'Baron Munchhausen' and 'Bambini di Praga'. The context which ties one yarn to the next, and which is not something added from outside, but emerges almost spontaneously as the various mini-stories line up one after another, is ultimately such a powerful structural element that Hrabal can entirely give up on any traditional organisation of the narrative by *syuzhet*.

Where Hrabal came by this structural principle is, of course, obvious: he found it in his Muse, Uncle Pepin. In an earlier "transcript", *The Sorrows of Old Werther*, the various building blocks (the pub yarns) are often put so out of focus as to be barely "legible", yet the sheer power of the all-uniting voice of Pepin does somehow hold them together. And so it is certainly no accident that the crowning

---

60) See Roth: *Laute Einsamkeit*, p. 61.
61) Ibid., pp. 63ff.

text of this yarn-spinning phase is *Dancing Lessons for the Advanced in Age,* a spectacular monologue in which all the yarns are swept along by the mighty current of a single narratorial performance that has neither beginning nor end and is, conspicuously, an analogue of life itself.

VII

The last two of Hrabal's books from the late 1960s, *Gory-stories and Legends* and *Flower Buds*, did not amount, as already indicated, to a new departure, but were more a bit of personal literary archeology, a return to the beginning. By the time Hrabal had got these two manuscripts ready for printing, his desk drawer was almost empty and contained nothing new. The watershed nature of this moment was enhanced by the fact that in the atmosphere of embryonic normalisation, set in train by the Soviet occupation of Czechoslovakia in August 1968, Hrabal, an author beloved by readers and pampered by the critics, became – like dozens of other writers – a *persona non grata* in whose face the doors of publishers were firmly shut. In 1970, the bulk of the print run of *Flower Buds* was pulped (followed at once by *Domácí úkoly* [Homework], a book of reflections and conversations), after which Hrabal had to wait until 1976 to see another book published, and that only by ransoming his return to the literary scene by a compulsory act of self-criticism, which, unlike some others, he did with no hint of servility.

Thus, after 1970, Hrabal, whose works to date had come out in printings that ran into many thousands (the original collection of stories that came out in 1966 under the title *The World Cafeteria* had a print run of 102,000), became overnight an author with no chance of being published.[62] This happened at the very moment when he started to get his breath back and immerse himself in a period of reminiscing, the outcome of which was the two-part family saga *Postřižiny* (of which the established translation is Cutting it Short, August 1970) and *Městečko, kde se zastavil čas* (ditto, The Little Town Where Time Stood Still, March 1973) and an evocation of his bohemian years *Tender Barbarian* (autumn 1973). This switch to private retrospection, this return to childhood and adolescence, may be seen as a psychological reaction to the wretched state of the times, but it is questionable whether the writing of these texts really was primarily driven by a desire to escape to the security of a past that was immutable and lit by an idyllic light. The point is that

62) Published officially, that is. Editions of his works were published in Germany and Austria "without the author's knowledge or consent". They were on sale in the West and many copies were smuggled into Czechoslovakia. [DS]

one product of this second – truly meteoric – creative period was Hrabal's longest work in prose, *I Served the King of England* (summer 1970), and another the rhapsodic *Too Loud a Solitude* (completed in July 1976), that is, two texts that can emphatically not be described as "escapist".

This large body of prose (to be joined in 1978 by *Slavnosti sněženek* [The Snowdrop Festival] a collection of short stories, and by two more variations on the family theme at the turn of the 1980s, *Krasosmutnění* [Beautogriefery] and *Harlekýnovy miliony* [or *milióny*, Harlequin's Millions]) undoubtedly represents a new season in the chronology of Hrabal's works, on the levels of both subject matter and narrative style. However, closer inspection reveals that the change is more a product of the adoption of a new slate and that it certainly does not disrupt the underlying continuity of Hrabal's work.

In terms of subject matter, the most conspicuous feature is the shift towards the Proustian memoir that marks out the first two texts in this series. Lurking beneath that choice one can also discern something rather more momentous: the erstwhile "recorder" of the things that people say has begun now to record his own story, albeit half-hidden behind the stories of those who were closest to him early in his lifetime: his mother, stepfather and a third family member, Uncle Pepin. There are but fleeting glimpses of Hrabal the child and teenager here, but it remains the case that these are the first times ever in his writing that we are admitted to a degree of intimacy with him. In theory, we already know the people he is telling us about since he launched into a degree of reminiscing about his family in several stories from back in the 1950s and 1960s; here, only he is a new character. And although we only glimpse him here and there, we cannot forget for a second that this is the person who, as a child, saw and stored all these images. The diffident "recorder", who even quite recently had been "bashing himself into things and people", is now visibly present on the narrative stage in his own right, not hidden from view, but stepping back out from the things and people he is talking about.

The slapstick verism that combined different people's spun yarns into a collage has been abandoned in favour of an unparalleled monologue, which stands up thanks solely to the narrator. All this does mean, however, that Uncle Pepin's interminable sentence, as we know it from *Dancing Lessons for the Advanced in Age*, has won the day. The shift that has taken place resides in the fact that in *Dancing Lessons* the monologue had been staged: the person who had recorded it was not the same as the person speaking, therefore there had been no problem over the stylisation of the latter, including all the deviations from standard Czech that are tolerated in the spoken language. This theatrical effect has now been annulled, yet the tellers of these stories have retained the "non-literary" quality of their personal speech patterns, albeit at a less radical pitch. If Hrabal – following in the steps of Jaroslav Hašek – had systematically reduced the distance between colloquial diction and the demands of literary stylisation (and he had quite shocked readers of his first texts by the "sloppiness" of his narrative style), his case against *bon usage* has acquired a measure of magnanimity: his sentences are replete with, often incongruous, parentheses, overburdoned with relative clauses, and blithely awash with anacolutha. Yet the expressive effect of the licence so taken is immense: the sentences retain to perfection the emotional force that marks out the discourse of yarn-spinning, a discourse in which an actual experience that is being reported on is relived directly. Hrabal ultimately succeeded in forcing this adaptation of the oral "stream" (a term with which he liked to operate, sometimes also translated as "flow") on readers and critics alike and in so doing he left his not inconsiderable mark on how Czech narrative prose was to develop, his "reform" soon becoming something found worthy of imitation. Thus Uncle Pepin's lectures, which were far more important to Hrabal's quest than any kind of literary inspiration that might spring to mind, such as the automatic writing of Surrealism or the sentence as found in William Faulkner, were soon to find their eager and competent converts.

Milan Jankovič sees in this orientation towards the "text as stream" the abandonment of the recent poetics of Hrabal the recorder. This renders properly visible the watershed in Hrabal's output that came with the turn of the 1970s; but it is equally possible and proper to render visible the *continuity* between the two phases. The concept of the "text as stream" surely has roots not only in *The Sorrows of Old Werther* of way back in 1949, but also in the primal enchantment with Apollinaire's associative *zone* that directed Hrabal's poetic beginnings. As for the "poetics of the recorder", it is certainly true that the Hrabal of *Cutting it Short* and *The Little Town Where Time Stood Still* was giving up on identifying anonymously with things and other people's voices and returning to his own self, to a subjectivity buried beneath the "fallen leaves of sentimentality". But is it not the most intimate task of any recorder to set down that which he alone can set down, namely his own story and those of his nearest and dearest? That both texts did indeed arise from an awareness of this task is corroborated by Hrabal himself in a gloss to *Cutting it Short*:

This text is a chronicle about my mother, father and uncle. While they were still of the material world, they kept such a tight grip on the keys of my typewriter that I found no reason to chart the poetic quality of their lives. Today my hands are no longer tied and I'm amazed to realise that I am more old than young, that there is, then, a danger in procrastination, and that I and I alone can give a report on the brewery and the little town where time stood still. I have been inspired by the aviatic [*sic*] style of Chagall's paintings, and I have complemented the poetics of a recorder and editor of prodigious external events with an internal model of longing, and that has permitted me to metamorphose into a young woman and shine the torch of imagination into the past and bring to mind a certain sector in which a beautiful woman, now swallowed up by remorseless time, can be rescued.[63]

Hrabal acquitted himself to perfection: he turned his mother Marie, stepfather Francin and uncle Pepin into characters who now each live a life of their own in the consciousness of millions of readers. He pitched all his models of them heroi-comically: while he highlighted all their foibles and manias, he also gave free rein to his longstanding predilection for lyrical monumentalisation, as pointed out in his day by Václav Černý.[64]

---

63) 'O Postřižinách', *Proč píšu* [Why I write], in *SSBH*, Vol. 12, p. 308 (trans. DS).
64) See Václav Černý: 'Za hádankami Bohumila Hrabala, pokus interpretační' (1975), in Idem: *Eseje o české a slovenské próze*. Prague: Torst, 1994, pp. 89–133 (130).

Černý also captured brilliantly the more deeply seated causes that led Hrabal on, as he first dipped into his personal case history, to the image of his mother. "All the lyrical tenderness that we descry in the final stage of his work goes arcing back to an image of his mother as its source; the drama of Hrabal's reminiscing on his childhood paradise, his *recherche du temps perdu* that has remained vivid for many a long decade, ends in his mother's lap. [...] The world of this poet is, ever more evidently and just as invisibly as in the sincerely comprehensible hints at it, dominated by the primeval, part instinctively biological, part emotionally moral, mystique of the return to progenitrixes: he is hooked on his mother's womb."[65]

This mother fixation is the deepest-seated spring that makes *Cutting it Short* into one great hymn of praise to the *ewiges Weibliche*, and it carries all the more conviction for being sung from within, by the voice of an actual woman, the voice of an *anima*. Here, for the first time, Hrabal had earnestly attempted to portray a feminine outlook on the world, typified by a subtler responsiveness to an essential, instinctive sense for connections and by a natural gift of empathy, and the evocative force with which he was able to convey this outlook certainly tells us something of consequence as regards his own psychological make-up. As we know, he returned to it more than once, but the one singular modification of it is the part of the older Marie, now looking back on her life, in *Harlequin's Millions*. And it says a lot that at the very moment when he decides to talk about himself – as he launches into *In-house Weddings* – he is to mirror his self-portrait in the critical, but ever-understanding view of his wife.

An *anima* is closer to the world: it experiences the world to a greater depth, its responses to it are immediate, and the more intense for being so, and its most intrinsic gift is its aptitude for amazement. Marie is a kind of Sezession-iste vestal capable of changing the most ordinary things into mysterious celebrations of life. Hrabal's lyrical vision always tended to extract an everyday item from the flow of time and demonstrate its archetypal structure and almost divine potential. And for a woman – as Hrabal sees them – the ritualisation of the most mundane operations of things is a simple

65) Černý: 'Za hádankami', p. 132

matter, almost a matter of course. It is this ritualisation of life that makes it one never-ending celebration, and it is one of the main themes of *Cutting it Short*.[66]

On the very first page of the text there is a protracted ritualisation of the image of Marie and her husband meeting in the evening, at the table and by the light of an oil lamp, and of family intimacy generally (she is encoded here as woman–guardian of fire):

> I love my burning lamps as by their light I bring the plates and cutlery to the table, or newspapers or books are opened, I love lamp-lit hands as they rest casually on the table cloth, human hands, chopped off at the wrist, in the script of whose wrinkles one may read the character of the person to whom the hands belong... [...] ... every evening we would stand beneath the burning droplight, its green shade so huge that we could both fit under it, it was an umbrella-like device under which we would stand amid the deluge of the paraffin lamp's hissing light, I'd have one arm round Francin and be stroking the nape of his neck with the other, his eyes would be closed and he'd be breathing deeply, and, his calm restored, he'd put an arm round my waist and so it looked as if we were about to do a ballroom dance, but it was more than that, it was a cathartic ablution...[67]

A little further on there is an exuberant image of a hog killing, an emblematic, saturnalian image of death that sustains life (this time Marie is encoded as a bacchante):

> I held out a pail and those lovely entrails came tumbling into it, that symphony of wet colours and shapes, nothing left me so ecstatic as light-red pig's lungs, beautifully inflated like rubber bellows, there's nothing coloured that so matches the passion of the dark-brown of liver, tricked out with the emerald of gall... [...] I dug my hands back into the blood and broke into a run, several times Mr Myclík dodged out of the way,

---

66) The Czech name of the work, *Postřižiny*, actually suggests this aspect of celebration, thanks to one of the functions of the ending -*iny*, cf. *narozeniny* 'birthday' or *křtiny* 'christening'.

67) *Postřižiny*, in *SSBH*, Vol. 6, pp. 7–92 (9, 11–13), hereafter *Postřižiny* and page number (trans. DS, given that James Naughton's published English translation [see Literature] is not an exact match).

like dancing a Savoyard, then I daubed his face with blood and carried on skewering the black puddings, and I laughed as I fixed my eyes on the butcher, who was laughing with a healthy, hearty laugh, not just your ordinary laughing, but a laughter that reached back to pagan times, when people believed in the power of blood and spit...[68]

And to make it three, we suddenly have a description of ritual hair-combing (Marie as Aphrodite):

As long as my hair was wet, it held no promise at all of what started to happen to it as it dried; the minute it started to dry, it was as if thousands of golden bees had been born in those streaming drifts, thousands of fire-flies, as if thousands of little amber crystals had started to crackle. And when Boďa first ran a comb through my mane, there was that crackling and the hair sparkled and billowed and grew in volume and vibrancy...[69]

Marie plays all these female roles impeccably, and more besides: she immerses herself in the waves of a wooden vat inside the malt-house like a water nymph, and she joins Uncle Pepin on a climb to the wind-swept top of the brewery chimney in a "lyrico-comical parody of the Ascension".[70] She is an embodiment of the very an-archy of life, she is the bed in which a stream of metamorphoses flows, "adores chance and every unforeseen event and wondrous encounter",[71] and she is ever willing to begin anew, to start a "new life".[72] Against this streaming feminine principle Hrabal erected a masculine principle broken down into the alternatives of the proper, responsible and taciturn Francin and the crazy, irresponsible and garrulous Pepin.

Francin treats his marriage as both gift and burden: he would dearly like to give some direction to the stream of his wife's meta-morphoses (he is at his happiest when illness steps in and takes care of that function for him), calm her nerves and "temper all that

68) Ibid., pp. 17, 19.
69) Ibid., p. 22.
70) Černý: 'Za hádankami', p. 131.
71) *Postřižiny*, pp. 7–92 (78).
72) See *The Little Town Where Time Stood Still*, trans. James Naughton, London: Sphere Books (Abacus), 1993, p. 259.

goes on in life".[73] His ideal is a life consisting of regularly repeated, entirely predictable segments of the daily round (so he, too, is an architect of rituals, the rituals of the commonplace). He loves order: his ideal image of it is found in the perfectly tuned engines of cars and motorbikes. However, this Francin – an engineer à la Daedalus – does not exhaust all the possibilities of the masculine world: these only become fully manifest with the counterpoint that is his brother Pepin, a picaresque simpleton and constantly laughing carnival clown, representing the Dionysian alternative. Pepin is "womanishly" intoxicated by chance and by unforeseen encounters and vents his enthusiasm in Homeric laughter and endless tirades delivered at the top of his voice.

If Hrabal, who has inherited aspects of both sides, ever has to choose between these two attitudes to life, he opts for Pepin:

> ... but I knew that the Lord God didn't actually love the truth so much, in fact he loved madmen, crazy exalted enthusiasts, people like my Uncle Pepin, the Lord God loved to hear untruth reiterated in faith, he adored the exalted lie more than the dry unadorned truth, which Dad tried to use to blacken Uncle in my eyes, and in the eyes of my mother, who could get up to such silly tricks with my uncle that the tears would trickle down my cheeks and I would go into fits of laughter, and sometimes there came a kind of crunching in my eyes and my head, when I got the feeling that any moment a miracle would happen in our kitchen and St Hilary from the square would appear unto us, our patron saint of healthy laughter.[74]

It is the Dionysian pole, set most deeply in the fecund chaos of life, that must be preserved, Hrabal believes, if beauty is not to disappear from life. The fair-minded Francins of this world may indeed help to improve it and set it to rights, but they cannot save it. Francin himself knows as much: the moment Pepin, gradually enfeebled by age, falls silent, he takes over his part and starts gourmandising; his voice grows louder, he has fits of anger and he shouts a lot.

73) *Postřižiny*, p. 37.
74) *Little Town*, p. 160.

To put it another way: not only does the Dionysian myth come alive in Pepin, but so too does the Christ myth. Pepin takes upon his shoulders everything that others – cautious, decent citizens – have suppressed in themselves and he redeems their traumas through the laughter of a God's fool.

> And people would invite him into their homes, introducing their daughters and wives to him, because every citizen needed to fool about a bit, but none of them knew how, so Uncle Pepin did it for them, and people were grateful to him for it.[75]

A similar stylisation is accorded to Vladimír Boudník, the protagonist of the prose memoir *Tender Barbarian*; the first edition of its original text appeared only in 1990 in Czechoslovakia, though a "pirate" edition had appeared previously abroad, some copies of it being smuggled into the country. This is another work recalling the 1950s and Hrabal's time in the Libeň underground, and is another grand apotheosis of a Christlike-Dionysian fool.

Boudník, a qualified turner, factory worker, a hysteric of constantly "agitated senses" and a self-taught graphic artist bewitched by art, is redrawn here – with reference to the Goethean amalgam of poetry and truth (*Dichtung und Wahrheit*)[76] – in an archetypal form in which the images of Christ and Dyonisos are further overlaid by those of Orpheus and Antaeus.

> Vladimír, a master of tactile imagination, forever dying, on his last legs, but only so that he can rise from the dead, rejuvenate himself, gather the strength to smash through a wall with his head, get across to the other side and then follow his umbilical cord back to the beginnings of all things, back to the first week of the creation of the world. So he was able simultaneously to be as old as the world itself and as youthful as the break of day, as a new-born leaf. [...] In his sheet graphics he re-endowed elements with the refined structure of their masses... He renewed a number of myths... The myth of Dionysos, the handsome

75) 'Rozdělený byt' (A divided flat), *Krasosmutnění*, in *SSBH*, Vol. 10, pp. 37–52 (49) (trans. DS).
76) See *Něžný barbar*, in *SSBH*, Vol. 6, pp. 197–274 (199).

drunkard who is the source of a creative act, and the myth of Antaeus, the tale of a hero who, if ever he grows weak, can only be restored to strength by touching the earth. Vladimír was thrilled by cement mixers and their innards, drums of melting bitumen, jackhammers, acetylene cylinders, whose flexible hoses and welding torches purr away quietly and emit a blue light...[77]

A typical attribute of these mystical connotations is, again, an emphasis on ritualised behaviour patterns:

> Vladimír would approach all things in a ritual, sacral manner. He would get to work half an hour early so as to have time to get ready for it, like a priest preparing for mass, when he received a letter, he initially couldn't believe it, so he went back to it and carefully re-read the address. Having established that the letter really was for him, he'd set it down on the table. Then he'd carefully wash his hands and open the letter with the greatest of care. Then he'd stroll about a bit, and finally sit down, put his glasses on and read it slowly, then fold it and then read it once again. And then he'd put it away in a little case to join the hundreds of other letters, the thousands of other missives.[78]

This text's groundplan is surprisingly simple: it is structured as a chain of anecdotes, a collage based on the simple principle of addition, and Hrabal himself describes it – spot-on as ever – as like road-works, dug up, bridged with hefty timbers and planks nailed hastily together. What makes it a highly unusual literary feat is, again, its lyrical breath: all its story fragments are conveyed through the voice of a cathedral cantor singing a requiem for a dead friend, a hymn of praise and a lament in one.

Here, too, Hrabal is a visible presence: he and Egon Bondy follow faithfully – like a pair of disciples – in the Master's footsteps, constantly amazed at his doings and sayings; from one perspective the text is also a gentle travesty of the gospels. But Hrabal's presence actually goes deeper: just as he was present in the portrayals of Uncle Pepin, Francin and his own mother (he headed *Cutting it*

---

77) Ibid., p. 207 (trans. DS).
78) Ibid., p. 223 (trans. DS).

Short with Flaubert's famous "Madame Bovary, c'est moi"), he is now a conspicuous presence in the highly realistic and highly fantastical portrait of his friend. Furthermore, this double exposure is something that goes towards typifying this phase in Hrabal's oeuvre, which reached its acme in *Too Loud a Solitude*, where the self-projection completely overlies the true prototype of the original Haňťa, one Jindřich Peukert (later on, in *In-house Weddings*, Hrabal will be speaking unequivocally about himself).

When Hrabal speaks of Boudník's capacity for amazement and empathy, he is also speaking of the mainsprings of his own work. And when he speaks of Boudník's tactile imagination and his Antaean need constantly to touch things, the most elementary things and the most mundane, those most sullied by life, he is speaking of his own "total realism". When he is describing how Boudník writes his diary, attached to his notebook "like a phone book chained to a phone box",[79] and is at great pains to follow the "through-flow" of images, he is giving an accurate description of his own "automatic" method. And as he formulates the basic theses of Boudník's work – "to drive the [fuel] mixture straight up to the spark plugs with no dispersion in the carburettor", "the raw material straight into the sphere of the transcendent", and "through subjective relationships to his beloved matter to penetrate to the objective spirit of the age",[80] it is perfectly plain that he is looking for the right words in which to put first and foremost his own creed.

With *The Tender Barbarian* Hrabal had returned to the 1950s. The wretched state of affairs in Czechoslovak society may be mirrored only marginally and through the eyes of the underground, which had gone its own way and ignored the window dressing of the prevailing ideology, but none the less Hrabal, in a remarkably straightforward manner, identified in Boudník a true son of the age (doubtlessly also speaking of himself in the same breath):

All the vices of the times passed through Vladimír: the impishness, the acting-up, the pathological petulance, allergies to this and that, play-

79) 'Deník psaný v noci' (A diary written at night), in *SSBH*, Vol. 6 (*Něžný barbar*), pp. 201–06 (201).
80) *Něžný barbar*, *SSBH*, Vol. 6, p. 208 (trans. DS).

ing the simpleton and imbecile, the dogmatism, the romantic melancholia...[81]

This also captures to perfection what distinguished the mythic Boudník from the no less mythical Maries, Francins and Pepins. Boudník's time is the 1950s; he cannot but accept the time as his. But when the 1950s impacted on the lives of Hrabal's parents, their world suddenly collapsed and they lacked the capacity to live in it. Their naïve and unbroken characters, their spontaneous, "playful" sensuality, their tortured sense of duty and their truth-telling craziness may have all proved their worth as solid values in the dark days of the Nazi occupation, but the new age was not going to enter into any kind of dialogue with them: in vain do they try to perform their old rituals, in vain do they attempt to be each other's stand-ins – nothing works the way it had. By some weird, incomprehensible syllogism, what had once been praiseworthy was changing into its opposite ("You were decent to us, and that has to count against you, because it meant that you blunted the edge of the class struggle, do you see?"[82]). Once magic formulae were now just ordinary words: when Francin said, at the end of *Cutting it Short*: "We'll begin a new life,"[83] he was opening the floodgates to the unpredictable adventures of the next stage in their lives, but when, in *The Little Town Where Time Stood Still*, the same words are repeated by Marie after the works council has expelled her and her husband from the brewery, it is merely a statement of a melancholy necessity. Uncle Pepin's death and his last words – "What's tae become of the love?"[84] – set the seal on the extinction of this world.

And a good thing too, said Dad to himself, everything returns to its origin, now I can see that time really has stood still and the new time has really begun, but I have only the key to the old times, and the one for the new is denied, and I cannot live in the new time anyway, because I belong to the old time, which is dead.[85]

81) Ibid., 207 (trans. DS).
82) *Little Town*, p. 258.
83) *Postřižiny*, p. 92.
84) *Little Town*, p. 191.
85) Ibid., p. 298.

It was indeed the 1950s that created the break constituting the boundary line between the two worlds of the generation of fathers and that of their sons. The world before the 1950s (key, as we have seen, to Hrabal's life and work), the world before the apocalypse, had, in the eyes of sons, come to a final halt, frozen into old colour prints of scenes that simmer in an unbroken, Arcadian timelessness. The caesura of the 1950s enabled Hrabal to see that time of memories in idyllic terms, that is, in a genre paradigm far, far removed from the erstwhile total realism (but which had been in preparation in some of the retro-stories of earlier collections, such as *Bambini di Praga*).

In *Beautogriefery* (1979), a set of prose pieces that reprocess the memoir material already stored away in *The Little Town Where Time Stood Still*, the idyll genre is put to use with even greater thoroughness. The book was born of a desire to offer a publishing house a publishable version of the original memoir (*The Little Town* did not appear in print on its home ground until 1991), and there can be no doubt that many of the changes made to the original material and reinforcing the idyllic quality were down to self-censorship; the wind of futility that the 1950s blew on the protagonists of *The Little Town* is missing from this version: it ends with the liberation of Nymburk by the Red Army and a dance duel between Pepin and the Russian soldiers. Unmistakably, however, *Beautogriefery* is no mere meeker and milder version of *The Little Town*, but a fundamentally different text, borne along by a different poetics: it is not conceived as a memory stream, but is thoughtfully plotted into separate, largely autonomous mini-chapters. The chapters are in turn divided into paragraphs, as is the rule in narrations built up in the normal way and reflecting the author's thought processes. The substance of the narration is extended to include reminiscences about a number of local, small-town, characters, portrayed here three-dimensionally – which also reinforces the link between this work and the genre naturalism of the late nineteenth century and its relish for depicting odd provincial characters. The past is now evoked as a series of neat, colour-print postcards being looked through by a child. The juvenile perspective is, in this new book, a more substantive structural aspect than it had been in *The Little Town*: this time the narrator explicitly points out that the child's eye view is being reprised for the additional reason of making perfectly clear just how deep in the past the depictions lie. Thus *Beautogriefery* needs to be rehabilitated as, above all, a genre experiment (as is indeed heralded by the curious neologism of its very title): it is a composition of idyllic elegies presented in a classicising spirit.

Hrabal had actually tested this genre model in his previous book, *The Snowdrop Festival* of 1978. This was a collection of pictures from near Prague, the Kersko forest range with its colony of second homes, where Hrabal owned a cottage. The form published was, however, a mere fragment of the original collection, containing only sixteen of the original twenty stories; the unbrushed whole only came out in Vol. 8 of the Collected Works (1993).

In its day, the collection caused something of a quandary: it seemed that this time the matter that Hrabal was subjecting to lyrical monumentalisation was too ordinary, and some disquiet was certainly stirred by the fact that he was shedding an idyllic light here on the then present-day, the grey age of 1970s normalisation (re-stalinisation). However, there can be no denying these texts their authentic motivation, entirely comprehensible in the light of how Hrabal's poetics had been evolving: here, too, we are faced with an image of a plebeian, "historically insignificant" milieu and the principle of "undiscriminating observation". Kersko is, alongside Nymburk, Kladno and Libeň, unquestionably a major chronotope in Hrabal's life, and it cannot be held against the "recorder" in him that he felt the need to leave us a record, in the form of a series of lyricised images, of this place too. To interpret these texts as a sop to the demands of the state's culture policy would be wrong: Hrabal was quite unable to contrive his writing in that way; all his texts are at core profoundly apolitical, and to the extent that they nevertheless bear accurate witness to their age, that is merely the reverse side of his paramount unwillingness to ideologise literature. Hence in *The Snowdrop Festival* the image of the colony of country cottages reflects, among others, a sociological fact that was particularly symptomatic of the 1970s: the widespread flight into the private sphere, an escape from the roles allocated to employees of the state. The aesthetic intensity of these texts is often considerable, and in the remarkable final story, *Rukověť pábitelského učně* (translated most recently as An Apprentice's Guide to the Gift of the

Gab), Hrabal again professed – and quite justifiably – his adherence to the main articles of his poetics.

Hrabal's family saga came to a climax in 1981 with *Harlequin's Millions*, a work that borrows barely anything from *The Little Town* and is actually a genuinely original work. Once again it is a long monologue, a long-drawn-out elegy by the elderly and lonely Marie, completely abandoned by her youth and beauty and living out her remaining years in an old peoples' home, in her memories and in a time that is dead. Marie is contemplating her own image from the remote past, the Marie of *Cutting it Short*, but she can also see things that had previously eluded her perception: the social dimension of her life, which she had taken for granted when it was by no means such a matter of course. For example, she recalls the timid, rustic servant girls who had been at her beck and call and any image of whom had been completely obliterated from *Cutting it Short*. And not even here can Hrabal be suspected of calculated social criticism as per the order of the day; more should it be recalled that, way back, the "insulted and humiliated" had been a theme of *Jarmilka*. The lyricism of these reminiscences ranges quite wide, also incorporating collage-like evocations of the history of Nymburk such as Hrabal had copied out from works by local contemporary witnesses and chroniclers, and there is even space in them for the naïve emotionality that once marked out Hrabal's early "Art nouveau tinkerings in verse":

> It's raining now, for the second day in a row it's raining at the retirement home, I sit by the window, drops of water stream down the windowpane, below me are the little town and the pink ramparts and the pink streets and the pink church in a blue haze of rain. It's raining, but in the western sky is a patch of pink light, somewhere out there the sun has already broken through the rain, it's the moment just before a rainbow appears, the air is filled with shreds of beige mist.[86]

In this way Hrabal distilled *The Little Town Where Time Stood Still* into two new, substantially independent, texts. Thus his regard to

---

86) *Harlequin's Millions*, trans. Stacey Knecht. Brooklyn NY: Archipelago Books, 2014, pp. 136–37.

the pressures of censorship paradoxically extended his bibliography by two essentially autonomous items.

It is appropriate to wonder in this connection just how far Hrabal's work published in the 1970s was distorted by editorial exigence or the constraints of self-censorship. The question is not entirely new: even texts published in the 1960s had to take some account of period standards (regarding not only the acceptability of certain politically still touchy subjects, but also material involving vulgarisms or descriptions of sexual behaviour). Only in the 1990s, with the publication of Hrabal's *Collected Works*, which capture all variants of his writings and thus enable us to judge what motivated individual shifts, have we been afforded a clearer insight into such questions.

However, the question is more complex than it appears at first sight. In reality, Hrabal was given surprisingly frequently to creating new version of older texts *without* being compelled to do so by extraneous circumstances, just for the sheer pleasure of storytelling. In her monograph on Hrabal, Susanne Roth advocated objectively distinguishing between "variants", that is, versions that were deliberately meant to facilitate publication, and "variations", versions not affected by self-censorship that arose out of "a spontaneous playful impulse".[87] She also made the necessary point that the boundaries between the two cases are never entirely clear. *Beautogriefery* and *Harlequin's Millions* are both variants as much as they are variations, but more than anything else they are texts that stand happily alone.

Hrabal obviously rewrote his texts with gay abandon and treated all their variants and variations as legitimate items within his oeuvre. That is not to say that critics should feel inhibited about passing judgement on the various versions: Roth is right to point out that Hrabal's stance was legitimated by his own poetics, and here, too, she recalled that Hrabal underpinned his narration with oral genres (the pub yarn, anecdote, reminiscences), that is, genres motivated by the sheer pleasure of storytelling as such, not by any need to communicate something new. For oral genres repetition and variation constitute their mode of existence, abbreviation and amplification being two basic, and equal, rhetorical methods.

---

87) Roth: *Laute Einsamkeit*, pp. 112-113.

As we know from Hrabal himself, the things he wrote in the 1970s and 1980s were usually done in one go: he would pump his accumulated ideas, stories and images straight into the typewriter,[88] then snip out or cross out anything that he thought might lead to a loss of tension. His deletions could often be on a grand scale: for example, the leftovers from the *In-house Weddings* trilogy, which he kept in storage (and entitled *To, co zbylo* [What's left] with the jocular subtitle *Odstřižky a postřižiny* [Offcuts and Shortcuts]), took up eighty pages in small print as reverently reproduced in the *Collected Works* (*SSBH*, Vol. 12). In reality, Hrabal could not have experienced any great dilemma when having to make deletions to satisfy others: he knew that his text was certainly not going to crumple just because this or that motif had to be deleted ex post (no matter how precious or aesthetically relevant it might be of itself). The poetics he had created was such that no deletions born of censorship or self-censorship could do any real harm.

88) See 'O tvůrčí metodě, židenické babičce a středoevropanství' (On my creative method, Židenice Grandma and Central-Europeanism), *SSBH*, Vol. 17, p. 240.

VIII

I Served the King of England emerged in the course of eighteen days in the hot summer of 1971; it was published in *samizdat* and exile publishing houses, the first edition on home soil, in 1982, as an internal publication of The Jazz Section, being judged a provocation and prompting reprisals against the publishers. It was written at a single stretch, "alla prima", as Hrabal often put it, just like *The Little Town Where Time Stood Still*. Hrabal provided a detailed account of his actual method in 'Zpráva o pitvě vlastní mrtvoly' (Autopsy Report on My Own Corpse):

> My texts come into being long before they're rattled off into the typewriter... [...] The time when images overwhelm me and create an unintended organon, that other nature, that time's the most beautiful. It can last for several months, sometimes several years... [...] Then that particular day, that particular hour and minute, I'll sit down at the typewriter, sort of limber up my fingers and wrists the way athletes do before they kneel down to run their race. And then I start writing my story, still in that zero state, but with a single spotlight that I cast sharply on the images that grab for each other from the first one on, follow on from each other, like when abattoir workers drive the animals for slaughter from a cattle van, sometimes the images overlap, leapfrog one another, but I can keep up and get them rattled off into the typewriter, and having registered that my through-put in pages is about one in ten, sometimes even five minutes, I keep on writing, though I never know what I've written, I have no way of checking... [...] Only after I've written the last line am I done with the typewriter, after the final image has rounded off my film show, for me and me alone... [...] Then when I pluck up the courage and sit down and pick up a pen, I start making corrections and additions and invariably I get drawn into my story [...] like the first inspector I go after the story of an event, and if anyone were watching me they'd see me now smiling, now frowning, now even shedding a tear, so affected am I by my *story* as its first reader.[89]

89) 'Zpráva o pitvě vlastní mrtvoly', *Proč píšu*, in *SSBH*, Vol. 12, pp. 312-17 (312-16) (trans. DS).

His description of this "automatic method"[90] confirms that the foundation of these texts was, yet again, an oral stream, signalled as such by the very first sentence: "Mark well what I'm about to tell you." Just as he had once, while recording *The Sorrows of Old Werther*, tried to keep pace on the typewriter with the words and images of Uncle Pepin, now he is trying to keep up, no less furiously, with his own authorial discourse. We have it on his own authority that ex post corrections to *I Served the King of England* were only minimal.

Hrabal keeps the narrator of *I Served the King of England* at arm's length: it is his monologue that shapes the narrator as an autonomous character. This proceeding is not to be taken for granted in Hrabal; on the contrary, the fabric of the narrators of his prose works is amazingly varied: the female narrator of *Cutting it Short*, for example, does also grow into a real character, but this is far less true of the narrators of *Harlequin's Millions* or *Too Loud a Solitude*, and even less in the case of *The Little Town Where Time Stood Still*, where we may indeed identify the child Hrabal in the narrator, but this *Ich* is consistently reduced to the bare narrative function – with the particular anomaly here that although the reminiscences cover roughly three decades, what we hear throughout is the same voice of a child.

The task of the narrator of *I Served the King of England* is, again, to reminisce, thus not only chronologically, but also typologically, this work has a link to the texts of his family saga. The difference is that this time it is no private *recherche du temps perdu*: it does not draw to the same extent on individual life experience. But nor is it a case of free fabulation. Just as Hrabal had once taken possession of the memories of Uncle Pepin, this time he has also taken charge – with a confidence that fascinates – of the memories of other people (as the *In-house Weddings* trilogy tells us, he drew the core motifs from the collective memory of his wife's kinsmen). The fact that the material is second-hand in no way detracts from the intensity of Hrabal's rendition, his extraordinary evocative skills remaining quite unaffected: the detail in his description of the hotels of Czechoslovakia's First

90) As he calls it in the Postscript to *Closely Watched Trains*, SSBH, Vol. 7, p. 188.

(interwar) Republic that we find in *I Served the King of England* is at least as good as the images of environments of which he had first-hand knowledge (the brewery, ironworks, railway, paper recycling plant etc.). Hrabal, who was not one to cover his tracks and was surprisingly willing to take interested parties behind the scenes of his writings, detailed the sources of these images during a talk at Stanford university (1989):

> My friends have always been the underlings in hotels and restaurants, and they still are. ... my wife, who they called Pipsi, well, I met her when she was working as the cashier in the Hotel Paris. [...] A great friend of mine was Mr Vaništa, he had a pub, but he did his apprenticeship also at the Hotel Paris, so actually, ever since I was a lad, when I used to go to the pubs in Nymburk till I swapped them for the ones in Libeň, and after that following my wife to various restaurants and then to pubs around Prague [...], over that string of years I picked up so many stories, so many events, so many details that once, when I went for a pint to Sadská [...], well the guy who was the manager of the Blue Star there [...] started on about how *he*'d begun. And he'd begun as a trainee selling frankfurters on Čáslav station...[91]

Yet again, then, the source is "things people say", though this time used not as segments of an authorial collage, but melded into a seamless oral stream.

I Served the King of England is described in its subtitle as a "short story", though it has been widely treated as his only novel; Hrabal eventually called it a novel himself and – metaphorically – a tennis match in five sets.[92] These days it has indeed become possible to call any longish text a novel (and Beckett's "novels" have taught us not to expect necessarily either plot or character), yet to query the status of Hrabal's work as to its genre is not otiose. Even taking into account the endless variability of the novel form, it is still striking how little this work, unlike, for example, *Closely Watched Trains*, answers to the structure of this "appropriated" genre. It really is structured more like a tennis match in five sets, each set bringing a different

91) *Z besedy na Stanfordské univerzitě*, in *SSBH*, Vol. 17, pp. 304–19 (317–18) (trans. DS).
92) 'Zpráva o pitvě', p. 316.

conglomerate of episodes which, as a rule, "are not *syuzhet*-forming" and are "far removed from the literary necessity of development" of a plot.[93] *I Served the King of England* is in fact no more a novel than *Cutting it Short* is.

All that binds it together is the person of the narrator. Admittedly, that might be a solid enough point to constitute a novel in the naturalist vein, reducing plot construction to a linear image of a single life. As a rule, however, this novel structure, following such models as Maupassant's *Une vie* or Svevo's *Una vita*, relies on painstakingly exhaustive analysis of the protagonist, while in *I Served the King of England* that does not apply: Hrabal's hero's character is anything but coherent: his very name, Dítě (Ditie in the established translation), meaning 'Child', speaks volumes in this respect. The main decisions that affect his life lack almost any psychological motivation: his rise through the ranks of the hotel business is down to the "deus ex machina" Mr Walden and, during the Protectorate, to his German wife, and likewise his shift towards a Franciscan humility in the final chapter.

Hrabal, who was surprisingly systematic whenever he touched on traumatic moments in Czech history, took as one of the topics in this work the problem of Czech collaboration with the occupying Germans. His view of collaboration is by no means indulgent (in fact it is unsparing: the fruit of a collaborationist misalliance is a mentally defective child), but we could scarcely interpret the hero's problematical role on the historical stage in existential terms as "a test failed" or in ethical terms as "treason". His lack of psychological definition, which makes it impossible to state how far he is directly responsible for his actions and how far these actions are the inadvertent result of a chain of random impulses, constantly obscures the moral tenor of the story.

The protagonist-narrator's immaturity has much in common with Miloš Hrma of *Closely Watched Trains*: both have a difficult time entering life through the gateway of teenage eroticism and both willingly hand the dominant role to a woman; both are faced with the same historical situation, both exhibit a juvenile insecurity

---

93) Miroslav Drozda: 'Hrabalův mýtus a děj', in: Milan Jankovič and Josef Zumr (eds): *Hrabaliana*. Prague: Prostor, 1990, pp. 89–94 (89).

at a crossroads in their lives; and both look up to their personal paragons, Hrma to Hubička the train dispatcher, Dítě to Skřivánek the head waiter. It is hard to tell what actually turned Hrma into a resistance fighter and Dítě into a collaborator. Dítě may indeed have some of the prerequisites: he is by nature a servant who dreams of becoming a master. However, his willingness to serve is not presented as a negative, nor is his dream an object of derision: there is actually something heroic about the petty little waiter aspiring to become a millionaire and so augment his life with the respect denied to him (that life had begun in his grandmother's small, dingy room beneath the baths, and with fishing dirty washing out of a mill race). But then he does not want to become a millionaire so as to be able to give orders: even as a prosperous hotelier all he wants is to give the best possible service. His dream is no better considered than his life choices: he is sustained by being constantly amazed, in thrall to how, time and again, "the incredible becomes real".

The waiter Dítě makes contact with reality through all his senses, but he is quite incapable of keeping it at a distance: his reflection of the world is supremely naïve and his outlook seems to be conveying a caricature (or censure?) of Hrabal's "undiscriminating observation": he is outraged by the brutal attacks of young Czech males on his "little Egerländerin" and he willingly recognises the right of the Germans to a Bohemian homeland, while at the same time seeing the German women who are expected, in a hotel above Děčín, to spawn a new generation of Teutons, as strapping Moravians, and pregnant Aryan women remind him of the beautiful hostesses in the *chambres séparées* of the Hotel Paris. He is an avid collector of endless images that mirror and overlap each other, without ever asking after their real sense.

In this way, the world comes across to Dítě – as it does to many of Hrabal's characters, regularly invested with a similar "naiveté" – chiefly in its ahistorical, ritual forms that point to mythical images. His enthusiasm for grand hotels is deep-seated and motivated by how they enable him not only to witness, but also to engineer such rituals, making him one of the demiurges of this fairy-tale world: an Arcadian world of plenty, love, eternal youth and merrymaking, where it is so easy to be happy. He is less interested in wealth than in having his ambivalent role recognised, he, Caliban, being Prospero at one and the same time: if the high point in the life of the head waiter, Skřivánek, was when he "waited on the King of England", Dítě's life reaches its apogee at the Rabelaisian feast where he waits on the Emperor of Abyssinia.

Dítě is more interested in the forms of reality than its contents: even hotels are but empty forms filled only by the contents that are their clients. But forms only live life to the full where "time has stood still", in the timelessness of an idyll. With the German occupation and developments after the war the hero's life is invaded by historical time, which assigns more meaning to contents at the expense of forms. The hero's relationsip with the fanatical Reich-German Liza ultimately leads to the doors of the Hotel Paris being closed to him for all time and brings the time of merrymaking to an end. The new times are also given to rituals, but have no real sense of them, imposing them from outside and so oddly distorting them: instead of wreathing a women's belly with sprigs of spruce, it demands the screening of sperm and ritual intercourse under the aegis of the Nibelungs. This strange, inauthentic time ends with a dual apocalypse: the collapse of the "thousand-year Reich", during which Liza perishes, and the Communist coup, which finally puts paid to the hero's attempt to retreat into the earlier idyll.

The finale deposits the protagonist in the desolate Sudeten borderlands, vacated by the expulsion of the Germans. Freed of all the forms that had kept his identity together, he is now a "nobody". He is dead to both past and present (not unlike Beckett's heroes or Pirandello's Vitangelo Moscarda) and he is bathed in his solitude by nothing but the waves of the present moment.

The road I maintained and patched with rock I had to crush myself – that road resembled my own life. It was filling up with weeds and grass behind me, just as it was overgrown with grass ahead of me. Only the section I happened to be working on at the moment showed traces of my own hand. [...] But I didn't want to be seen by human eyes any more, or praised for what I'd done – all that had left me. [...] [t]he more I worked, the more I saw that the maintenance of this road was the maintenance of my own life, which now, when I looked back on it, seemed to have happened to someone else. My life to this point seemed like a novel, a book written by a stranger even though I alone had the key to it,

I alone was a witness to it, even though my life too was constantly being overgrown by grass and weeds at either end.[94]

Set free now from his Schopenhauerian will, the narrator can offer but one thing: the book of his life ("written by someone else"). In an out-of-the-way pub he lets "these images from the past pass by" and goes into the inevitability of

asking yourself questions, inquiring of yourself, interrogating yourself, wanting to know the most secret things about yourself, accusing youself as if you were a public prosecutor and then defending yourself ...[95]

Like Beckett's heroes, this hero of Hrabal's also finally finds a final reason for living in talking: he too becomes a character-narrative. And he wins satisfaction: on Christmas Eve, the villagers he had talked to in the pub, crash their sledges through snowdrifts into his solitude to make sure of his story.

Unexpectedly, then, the point of this entire picaresque story is Hrabal's creed as a writer. The life story of an outsider gains sense by having been set down. The narrative is more important that the narrator and has its own ethics: it is always a portrayal of a truth. From this perspective, the question of who has actually been telling us the story (a good man or bad? guilty or innocent? foolish or wise?) dwindles in importance.

Literature – its fragility and its force – is also one of the themes in *Too Loud a Solitude*, one of Hrabal's most intricate, complex and profound texts. This work, too, is linked capillary-wise with numerous others (it uses reminiscence, spread over a full 35 years, no less; it contains evocations – so central to Hrabal – of the 1950s; and it also deals with the ultimate vacuity of rituals), but what makes it exceptional is its hugely accentuated metaphysical horizon. In this respect, *Too Loud a Solitude* is a denial of Hrabal's previously dearly adhered-to principle of "undiscriminating observation" with its

94) *I Served the King of England*, trans. Paul Wilson. London: Picador, 1990, p. 226 (amended DS).
95) Ibid., pp. 227-228.

deep-seated amoralism, and the ethics of this narrative is no mere ethics of the "true report", but also an ideal mission statement.

The history of this work is at once short and long and considerable attention has been paid to it (notably by Susanne Roth and Milan Jankovič[96]). Its genesis was rather more complex than in the case of *I Served the King of England*: evidence of this is the fact that from the very outset it has existed in three variations, two in verse and one in prose. On the other hand, we are undoubtedly dealing here with the spontaneity of authorial *diktat*, and Hrabal must surely have had good reason for dating all three versions alike: July 1976. And he did describe the work's genesis in *Autopsy Report on My Own Corpse*:

> ...the first version, which I wrote in a kind of Apollinairesque verse, perhaps so as not to have to bother with punctuation marks, but perhaps also because I saw the entire story in lyrical terms only...[97]

This version was re-written in prose:

> However, when I read the text for the first time, I discovered I'd written it in Prague Czech, not slang, but in colloquial speech. And suddenly it dawned on me that my motif of the ordinary man who has been educated, if against his will, lacks irony, and that Praguian irony can rise to the surface and that it will hit harder if put in meticulous, fussy standard Czech. So, full of excitement, I retuned myself and re-wrote *Solitude* in the style I'd set myself, and whether depending on the moment or from a natural slovenliness here and there I shifted the text a bit away from the original, or made just a slight alteration, because I knew that actually I couldn't do the text any harm, because I was afraid of it, and when I'm afraid of a text of mine, well, at the very least, it's a good one.[98]

However, it was another – and, it has to be said, surprising – version of *Solitude* that first appeared in Czech bookshops rather

---

96) See Roth: *Laute Einsamkeit* and Jankovič: *Kapitoly* respectively.
97) 'Zpráva o pitvě', p. 317 (trans. DS)
98) Ibid.

later, in 1981. This time, Hrabal, in a form of textual *prollage*,[99] inter-
wove *Too Loud a Solitude* with *Tender Barbarian*, also not published
previously, creating of them a new "variant" to which he gave the
title *Kluby poezie* (Poetry Clubs). In the process, he made, as an act
of self-censorship, a number of cuts that related – according to the
summary provided by Susanne Roth, who looked in great detail into
this problem – to the "topics of history and politics, the erotic and
sexuality, religion and philosophy".[100] The manner in which Hrabal
coped with the pressures of censorship was repeatedly castigated in
some critical circles, that is, unofficial, samizdat circles, and there is
no doubt that his concessions did impair the text. It would, however,
be wrong to take an entirely negative stance: leaving aside the fact
that Hrabal's desire to communicate with the reader was entirely
legitimate and that he had always been obliged to resort to some
degree of concessions, it should be recalled again[101] that Hrabal's
poetics allowed in principle for "eliminations and modifications" and
that his willingness to have this version published – "the greatest
compromise he ever embarked on" – does in the end indicate that
he felt able to stand by even this mutilated end-product (reader
reception confirmed he had done right). Nor is it really feasible to
see the merger of *Tender Barbarian* and *Too Loud a Solitude* as merely
a pragmatic, opportunistic experiment that sought to smuggle two
problematic texts into the bookshops at once: this peculiar prollage
in the manner of Faulkner's *The Wild Palms*, validated by Hrabal
himself with a shared Sisyphean metaphor, is undoubtedly an experiment to be taken seriously.

In the person of the hero of this work we see returning to the
stage the waste-paper packer Haňťa, the "Baron Munchhausen" of
Pearls of the Deep, though altered beyond recognition. While the
one-time yarn-spinner (Uncle Pepin's double) was clearly a highly
stylized portrait of his real-life prototype (Hrabal's colleague in the
Prague recycling plant, one Jindřich Peukert, known as Heinrich,

99) This is a pictorial, rather than written, technique, one amongst many ending in
-*age* and derived from *collage*, much employed by Jiří Kolář. For a little more on this
see http://modernistencaustic.com/portfolio-items/prollage/ and https://cs.wikipedia
.org/wiki/Prol%C3%A1%C5%BE (in Czech only). [DS]
100) See Roth: *Laute Einsamkeit*, p. 161.
101) cf. Roth: *Laute Einsamkeit*, pp. 167 and 176.

Heinie or Haňťa), his new look is largely an autostylisation of Hrabal himself:

> ...Haňťa was precisely the one who'd been educated against his will, in other words I compiled the story, and I quite pride myself on it, this *Too Loud a Solitude*, from him, also pasting onto it an autobiographical myth, so it's a kind of double-act that I've put together, Haňťa and myself, thanks to my education and that environment...[102]

What links this narrator to many of Hrabal's other characters is his isolation (this time announced in advance, in the title), from which he buys his release with his story-telling. *Too Loud a Solitude* speaks of the factual (autobiographical) loneliness of an ageing man whose purview is constantly shrinking; but it is also – as an "existentialist story" – another tale of an "Everyman", and from this perspective solitude is also an attribute of all human existence.

None the less, this version of solitude is still penetrated by the "noise" of life. Haňťa loves his job: as for the erstwhile "Baron Munchhausen", for him, too, work is that "platform where we brush against one another, while otherwise we are beyond one another's grasp", a space of "visitors and encounters", a crossroads of human stories and a site of carnival costume-changing (consider the game of the wicked boss and psyched-out worker that he plays with a myopic professor of philosophy). But his solitude is peopled even more loudly by the voices of books, the books that he is destroying, but that he also lets speak to him and that have so filled his world as to put him literally in peril of being pulped himself. And last but not least, Haňťa's solitude echoes to his memories, the still articulate voices of his own life-story.

On the one hand, this train of memories forms a link between *Too Loud a Solitude* and Hrabal's retrospections on his family, while on the other it makes Haňťa the story-teller into a three-dimensional character. Here, too, the various memory segments are not tied together to provide a consecutive *fabula*, but they do possess a remarkable depth and eloquence: it is they that evoke the "love" that Uncle Pepin was looking for in his final Pythic sentence, the

102) *Z besedy na Stanfordské univerzitě*, p. 319.

principle that shines through the impenetrable chaos of life, reconciling its unbridgeable contradictions and leading man into "the very centre of the Garden of Eden".[103] Haňťa remembers his Mančinka, whom malevolent fate cast time and again from the highpoints in her life down into an abyss of infinite mortification, but she was finally granted the blessing of "knowing her ignominy and preserving her glory";[104] and he recalls in particular the tiny Gypsy girl who never desired more than to listen to the melodic singing of the fire and who was finally consumed by fire in a furnace at Auschwitz. This evocation of the Roma holocaust (almost unique in Czech literature, and unique within Hrabal's oeuvre for the purity of its tender lyricism) is the most profound motivation for Haňťa's balladic monologue and the very wellspring of the leitmotiv of his lament – "the heavens lack humanity" – and its basic perspective: viewing things *sub specie mortis*.

Haňťa is unmistakably a part of the plebeian world of Hrabal's yarn-spinners: he, too, is an eternal outsider, a hostage to the banal, never-ending twists and turns of the irrationality of history. However, this time Hrabal takes the surprising step of binding his character to the imaginary universe of books, transplanting him, through them, into the realm of the spirit:

> When I get into a decent book with my eyes, when I set aside the printed words, then nothing more of the text is left than intangible thoughts that flutter through the air…[105]

This "ordinary man", Haňťa, "became educated against his will". He is a pitcher filled with the water of life and death, his solitude is peopled by thoughts, his life is (and this he shares with Beckett's heroes) "life in the spirit", and from the frontages of tenements he is capable of reading references to the "Greece within us". He is attended by his great masters, Jesus and Lao-Tze, the latter having a particular appeal to him thanks to his dialectic of paradox and

103) *Příliš hlučná samota*, in *SSBH*, Vol. 9, pp. 7-78 (77) (trans. DS; the published English version in Michael Heim's translation is based on a different, or hybrid variant of the original).
104) Ibid., p. 29.
105) Ibid., p. 10.

his understanding for the "insolubility of the moral situation of contradictions".[106]

The point here is that the world Haňťa inhabits is one more likely to be understood by Lao-Tze than Jesus. It is so riddled with absurd contradictions as to seem at times to have been turned inside out. A nation who "has known how to read for fifteen generations"[107] is constantly destroying books,[108] people with a university education are working as drain-cleaners, and workers are being sent to night school.[109] And by an irony of fate, Haňťa himself, reader and philosopher, is one of the golems whose task it is to destroy books.

Haňťa knows exactly when Adam (as the protagonist of this very work was to be called originally) was banished from the Garden of Eden, the heavens closed and the hurly-burly of mankind began to look like the perpetual, internecine warfare of clans of sewer rats. It had come about around the time when they incinerated the little Gypsy girl. And after the war Haňťa continued weeping at the sight of the Royal Prussian Library, its holdings getting rain-sodden in open railway wagons, but the 1950s hardened him and taught him (like Hrabal, like Boudník) a new sensibility: a Bretonesque delight in the beauty of destruction:

> Some years later I started getting used to it, I loaded entire libraries from stately homes and burgher houses, beautiful books bound in leather and morocco, I loaded truckfuls of them, and once there were thirty trucks, the whole train hauled the books off to Switzerland and Austria, a kilo of beautiful books for one Tuzex crown, and nobody batted an eyelid and nobody shed a tear...[...] By then I'd found within me the strength to look on at this tragedy impassively so that I could curb my emotions,

106) Ibid., p. 32.
107) Ibid., p. 10.
108) Hrabal has all the facts right where he recalls such historical bouts of this particular kind of iconoclasm as the postwar destruction of the Royal Prussian Library in Berlin and the destruction of monastic and aristocratic libraries in Czechoslovakia following the Communist takeover in 1948; what Haňťa is involved in is the scrapping of books that marked the start of the "normalisation" (re-Stalinisation) following the termination of the "Prague Spring" by the Soviet invasion of August 1968.
109) This is another authentic detail of the 1970s, which saw a re-run of what had gone on in the 1950s.

back then I was beginning to understand how beautiful the sight of devastation and disaster can be…[110]

If the heavens are not humane, man cannot be humane either. There is probably something more than these heavens, to wit compassion and the love of which Uncle Pepin spoke; but, as Haňťa says, "I've gone and forgot that now".[111] The only way left to Haňťa by which he can arrest the frenzy of time is that known so well to other Hrabal heroes: a ritual whereby chaos is transmuted into a cosmos. "By his chosen ritual, man creates an order that he can hold on to – perhaps because there are no other hard-and-fast values left in the world."[112] If the world lacks order, we have to find it within our own selves and re-implant it in the heart of things. That lesson was taught Haňťa by his Gypsy girl, and Mančinka also proved able, like a Muse, to initiate a ritual of creation that turned her into something that endures in defiance of time: a statue. And, likewise, Haňťa has his own ritual, one in which the course of destruction is arrested:

> But just as a beautiful little fish may glint in the tide of a muddy river that has come flooding through an industrial site, so too the spine of a beautiful book may glint in the tide of waste paper, dazzled, I look away, then I fish it out, wipe it on my apron, open it and sniff the text, and then like making a homeric prophecy I read the first sentence my eye alights on, and only then do I stow the book with other beautiful finds in a little crate lined with holy pictures […]. It's then my holy mass, my ritual, not only to read each such book, but, having read it, to pack it in this or that bundle, because I need to bedeck every bundle, I need to give it my character, my signature. […] So I'm the only one in the world who knows which bundle holds, as their burial chamber, Goethe and Schiller, which one Hölderlin, or Nietzsche.[113]

This ritual does more than confirm the transience of all material things: it also confirms the indestructibility of an idea. For a book

110) *Příliš hlučná samota*, p. 15.
111) "už jsem zapomenul a zapomněl", ibid., p. 52.
112) Roth: *Laute Einsamkeit*, p. 184.
113) *Příliš hlučná samota*, p. 12.

once read lives on in the memory, its life unquashable, it passes into the brain and heart and "rattles through the veins to the very roots of one's blood vessels".[114] The next time anyone felt like compressing books, he would have to compress heads.

> ... so all the world's Koniášes burn books in vain, and if those books have meant anything worthwhile, all you hear is their silent laughter as they burn, because a book worth its salt always points out and away.[115]

The typological link between *Too Loud a Solitude* and the books of memoirs is given by more than just the important role played by reminiscence: like the latter, *Solitude* is also no funerary lament over the end of the good times. In Haňťa's case, the key turning point is the introduction of extremely powerful monster presses. The arrival of his own new press meant the arrival of new people, people dressed in clean overalls and with gloves to wear as protection from contact with books. And the advent of "socialist work brigades" meant the end of the "worker-proletarian" who had lived in perfect symbiosis with his work: the work may have left his hands chafed and filthy, but the pages of all the mashed-up books also begrimed his eyes and heart. The new people keep their job literally at arm's length, working "unfeelingly and unhumanly": they are at no risk of acquiring an education "against their will". They do not experience the world, they just use it; their reading of books tells them nothing of the world's spiritual dimension, the dimension of beauty, truth and love; Greece, which for Haňťa is an inner experience mediated by Aristotle, Plato and the façades of the tenements of Žižkov, is, for them, just the backdrop of their holidays.

Much as Uncle Pepin fell silent in this world, so Haňťa has no desire to live in it either. He steps down inside his baler (in the last variation of *Solitude* in his sleep, in the two earlier version quite literally) in order to become a sacrificial victim on the altar of a ritual

---

114) Ibid., p. 9.
115) Ibid. The Koniáš of this quotation is Antonín Koniáš (1691–1760), a fanatical Jesuit of the Counter-Reformation who drew up a list of proscribed works and is said to have ordered the burning of around 30,000 books. [DS]

mystery. In that instant, the character of the Christlike simpleton Haňťa merges finally with his archetype: by his death he wipes out the trials of the world, which had crossed the bounds of the bearable, and his face climbs up into the sky along the string of a paper kite, held in her tiny hands by the long-dead Gypsy girl.

IX

In 1982 Hrabal churned out a 700-page typescript provisionally entitled *Svatby v domě aneb Život bez rukávů* (In-house Weddings or Life Without Sleeves), which he described in the subtitle as "texts from a diary". In it he "recorded" the history of his marriage: this amounted to the erection of a touching monument to his wife Eliška, née Plevová (1926–1987), any portrait of whom had previously been missing from his writings, though they had drawn into their magical field everything else that girdled his life.

The story begins somewhere in 1954, with the moment when Eliška first bumped into her future husband on the staircase of the house in Libeň where he was living at the time, and ends with his leaving that house in 1973. So, once more, it contains a history of the 1950s, Hrabal's transformation into a writer during the 1960s, and the distressing period of his ostracisation in the first years of Normalisation after August 1968.

This "memoir" is in many respects unique. Its very bulk is surprising: Hrabal had never once hinted that his ambition was to produce a statement of such breadth. Even more surprising, however, is the confidence of his diction. Although it is obvious that this text was anticipated by the prose reminiscences of the 1970s, and that we have before us, yet again, a literary transformation of an oral stream, we cannot fail to observe that Hrabal's poetics of the fluid monologue is materialised here with unprecedented grandeur and facility. The text's composition is again loose in the extreme, but the narrator – Hrabal's wife Eliška herself – keeps it in check by the extraordinary power of her voice, her unifying perspective; the impression here is not of a dug-up street hastily bridged with planks, as it had been with *Tender Barbarian*. The reasons for this intensification of the narratorial voice are not far to seek: none of Hrabal's previous narrators had been endowed with the same complex, psychophysical consistency, none was metamorphosed into such a delicately drawn character. Also unique to this text is the bluntness of the attack on the perversion of the age, though that should come as less of a surprise, since there were elements of the same in all of Hrabal's works dealing with the 1950s or 1970s.

The originality of the text is somewhat veiled by the fact that much of the material in previous works – Libeň, Boudník, the Hotel Paris, the destruction of books in a recycling plant, and, in flashbacks, Hrabal's mother, stepfather Francin and Uncle Pepin – is here again. In fact, however, the material here present is fundamentally new. Everything that has been told somewhere before is now shunted into the background, the foreground being reserved for two entirely new stories: Eliška's and that of "the doctor", that is, Hrabal himself. Although Hrabal had been writing mainly about himself since the 1970s, he had so far projected his own features – as already noted – into portraits of others, by donning various masks: this is how he had been present in the portraits of both Francin and Pepin; the portrait of Boudník was inscribed with a self-portrait; his clearest self-projection was in Haňťa in *Too Loud a Solitude*, and many a personal quirk doubtless also went into such a psychologically hard-to-grasp hero as the protagonist of *I Served the King of England*. This time he has decided to cast aside such narrative masks. Yet he still has not shed quite all the inhibitions holding him back from making a direct confession, hence entrusting all the talk of himself to his wife: it is as if he thought it more merciful to have himself portrayed in the voice of an *anima*.

This mirroring is, in fact, a stroke of genius: Hrabal is reminiscing on how he has seen his wife over their twenty years together, whereas the topic of the reminiscing is formulated in reverse: "how my wife has seen me." Thus the first-hand experience of a memoir is discreetly transformed by the virtuoso narrative game being played: with perfect empathy, Hrabal constructs the precise perspective of a female view that he allows to alight on himself.

The sheer ease with which this text is mastered is surely a reward for the many years that he had devoted to writing, but it is no mere resting on the laurels of the ultimate certainty he had about his personal poetics: there is still an element of surprise in just how far this text remains imbued with its author's keenness to experiment. The manuscript acquired its final version in the course of 1984–85, when he returned to it, meaning to rework it into a trilogy, the different parts of which have remarkably dissimilar, distinctive formal structures. The first part, called *In-house Weddings*, had the subtitle "A Romance for Girls" tacked onto it, and Hrabal, in a long monologue by his wife, really was parodying here the "appropriated structure" of a trash novel telling the tale of a broken heart that finds happiness in a new love. And logically, in harmony with the genre, this part ends in a wedding. He gave the second part, *Vita nuova*, the subtitle "kartinky" (basically 'pretty pictures', a Russism): it is the longest and most remarkable section, "pictures" of the marital daily round being literally swept along by the oral stream, whose "flow-rate" is increased by the omission of punctuation. In the third part, entitled *Proluky* (Gaps) and beginning with Hrabal's entry onto the literary stage at the start of the 1960s, he attempted to restore some rhythm to the oral stream by breaking the text down into shorter segments that generally start with an anaphoric "my husband...".

In the first part, *In-house Weddings*, Hrabal's past and that of his wife-to-be are intertwined in a brilliant counterpoint. In numerous retrospectives, Eliška the narrator provides a detailed reconstruction of her past. But this is more than an intimate tale of the unrequited love of a girl from a good family: through the prism of Eliška's memories, Hrabal again recalls – as in *I Served the King of England* – the chequered modern history of a large proportion of Czechoslovakia's Germans (from the pro-Hitler mood of the 1930s to the tragedy of their post-war expulsion), doing so with an eloquence quite unmatched within Czech literature. Parallel retrospectives evoke in turn the story of "the doctor", commencing in the affluent idyll of the Nymburk brewery and ending in the pubs of Libeň and the waste-paper processing plant.

The developing intimacy of the two protagonists is presented as their mutual exposure and the cross-permeation of the two pasts: the moment at which the two pasts arrive and from which they slash their way into a common future is, once again, the beginning of the 1950s, an age that all these memories have hurled "into the abyss of time". The prewar idyll is brought back to the protagonists at every turn – by abandoned outdoor restaurants, the tenants of the Libeň house, publicans from the First Republic – but they are all but dim reflections of something that has gone forever: the new age "doesn't like this level of beauty".[116] Thus a core theme of this text is

116) *In-house Weddings*, translated by Tony Liman. Evanston IL: Northwestern University Press, 2007, p. 62 (hereafter *In-house Weddings*).

the lifestyle transformation that came with the 1950s: an imposed, but accepted "melancholy apocalypse".

I mean to say, it's as though a board broke and we are caught in the splinters of the break, the splinters pierce us, stick in our bodies - so all the while we have a view of the calamity... Don't regret a thing anymore, anything you once had, everything Liza let me know about, all gone, lost, and all you can do is look on it with pride, you can look down on your fall, but you must always look up, [...][117]

... you see, we live in a time ashamed of its past, that's why it's attempting to cover its tracks, as a young girl destroys love letters, when she marries someone other than the correspondent who wrote her so beautifully...[118]

Smoothly integrated into Eliška's monologue are utterances spoken by both main actors, their dialogues, microscopic descriptions of exteriors and interiors, and evocations of simple actions, usually broken up into separate short shots. Eliška tells her story at an easy pace, evincing a gift for seeing things in precise detail, often as if this were a return of the naturalist *Sekundenstil*,[119] in which the time narrated merges with the time of the narration. Hrabal's style is ideally suited to the subliminal theme of this text, to wit, the flow of time lived.

I changed into my bathing suit and just sat there a while, dipped my foot in, then felt for the sandy bottom, the water was alive, the darling water tugging, I stood up, then waded carefully in, water up to my knees, my waist, I splashed my chest lightly, then took a few steps more and water was up to my chest, I dove in and started to swim, the water carried me, lucky I was one for water, too, knew how to swim, my only sport, I took one, two strokes and made it back to shore, probed for the sandy bottom, stood and washed my face in the sweet-scented water, then looked toward the sluice, the doctor readying the inflatable, he lay down on it,

117) Ibid.
118) Ibid., p. 91.
119) *Sekundenstil* (generally not translated) is a narrative technique within Naturalism, promoted by Arne Holz and Johannes Schlaf. [DS]

and the running water bore him down over the sluice, the red-and-blue mattress tore along the falling waves, and the doctor raised his arm, I raised my arm and waved, then froze, because the mattress was picking up the speed of falling water and hurtling, about to burst through a set of rapids and finally emerge from a flurry of water, right in front of me.[120]

By suppressing the punctuation in the immediately following text, *Vita nuova*, Hrabal cast an even sharper light on this *Sekundenstil*. In this part Eliška is reporting on the first years of her marriage to "the doctor". If their pathways in the first section had gradually grown closer, here divergences start to show. The marriage was brought to an end by Hrabal's bohemian years: his wife, using coloured threads to weave pictures of Prague Castle and Lüneburg Heath and reading aloud the poems of Bohdan Kaminský from *Zlatá Praha*,[121] was too much for Hrabal's "non-conformist" friends, admirers of Ezra Pound, beatniks and *art brut*. For all that, the leitmotif of this section is Hrabal's tormented realisation that he was incapable of fulfilling his creative destiny. The time that passes here is a time squandered non-stop. Hrabal's inability to stand by his mission is continuously ironised by his mother, sarcastically carped at by Boudník, reproachfully criticised by Kolář and compassionately accepted by his wife.

In *Gaps* Eliška describes how her husband did finally become a writer and what the consequences were. In this final text, her view of her husband begins conspicuously to overlap with Hrabal's mother's view of her son. At the end of this third section his stepfather Francin dies, as does his Uncle Pepin and Vladimír Boudník, and the atmosphere is fraught with the ideological monitoring of culture and the police monitoring of its exponents.

Each of the three parts depicts a clear-cut period in Hrabal's life, and each depiction is, as noted, evoked by an original modification of Eliška's monologue. However, no matter how differently

120) *In-house Weddings*, p. 68.
121) *Zlatá Praha* – an illustrated magazine founded by the poet Vítězslav Hálek, appearing fortnightly in 1864-65 and weekly between 1884 and 1929. It contained chiefly literature, but also included commentaries on current affairs in politics and culture and reproductions of works of art. [DS]

each monologue is stylised, they do have one feature in common: the strikingly lyrical flavour of the Hrabal sentence. A tendency to endow a prose sentence with a lyrical quality is certainly not new in Hrabal: it has been there ever since *Cutting it Short* and in the balladic monologue of *Too Loud a Solitude* it is quite striking (but then, as we know, underlying that work is a version written in verse). However, it is only in the trilogy that it becomes the main principle governing the style.

Milan Jankovič, who has paid considerable attention to the sentence in Hrabal, has shown[122] that while ordinary discourse that aspires to clear expression of semantic and grammatical relations is typified by heterogeneous intonation, Hrabal builds up his sentence by constantly breaking it down into segments typified by rhythmical analogies, exploiting simultaneously the traditional poetic procedures of parallelism, repetition and gradation (and, in *Gaps*, also anaphora).

Hrabal's return to the lyrical methods mastered during his youth as a poet was doubtless conscious and deliberate: he himself is alluding to the lyrical rhythmisation of his stream in *Gaps*, when he has Eliška comment on his awkwardness when giving talks:

> ...his voice quavered, like he was being throttled, and thus he went on, until finally catching the flow of his thoughts, and then it was like he was narrating a story just one-on-one, and he forgot all about the audience and suddenly hit his stride, like when he wrote and things went well, everything flowing in time to his own breathing ...[123]

Jankovič's insight also revealed that the way Hrabal handles punctuation here always has the same function: to point up the rhythmical segmentation of sentences. Hrabal's punctuation is often redundant, going beyond the rules prescribed by standard Czech syntax so as to mark out rhythmical units as well:

122) Jankovič: *Kapitoly*, p. 123.
123) *Gaps. A Novel*, translated by Tony Liman. Evanston IL: Northwestern University Press, 2011, p. 50 (hereafter *Gaps* and page number).

Then Ludva asked me to dance, he didn't make the full circles when we danced the waltz together, he just swayed to the rhythm, held me so tight I was only able to loll in his arms, he was looking at me closely, very closely, the exact opposite of the doctor, who always averted his eyes as if guilty of something, as he always said about himself, he was shy, because when he was a youth the custom was that young men be shy.[124]

But this rhythmical segmentation is even more striking whenever Hrabal abandons punctuation altogether, since if the reader is to find his bearings within a sentence's semantic structure, his main guideline is its rhythm (insofar as the role of punctuation has not been taken over by the repetition of conjunctions, most notably the anaphoric *and*):

I finally decided to bite the bullet and do a huge load of laundry for the first time in my life My husband requested a day off like I was ill or like we were having another wedding or a divorce or a death in the family and in the end I was glad he helped me soak the laundry and draw a clothesline across the courtyard and light a fire under the cauldron in the laundry room first thing in the morning that was his thing he just couldn't get enough of the fire roaring under the cauldron and it was my stuff that went into the Swedish washing machine first and my husband went from the courtyard to the flat and got the stove in there going as well... I was glad he worked as my fireman and he smiled and launched into a lecture that he should have saved for himself he tried to tell me that writing wasn't all that hard that it didn't take much more than a healthy dose of arrogance to get down those first few lines and then it just ran on its own like a thread from an old sweater coming apart at the seams...[125]

Hrabal himself says something about the poetics of these texts in the foreword to *Vita nuova*, where he also tenders a surprising instruction on how the texts should be read, telling us thereby something material to his attitude to literature:

124) *In-house Weddings*, p. 78.
125) *Vita nuova*, trans. by Tony Liman. Evanston IL: Northwestern University Press, 2010, p. 30 (hereafter *Vita Nuova* and page number, unless stated otherwise).

Now I've completed *Vita nuova* a text I wrote in the stream of one long inhalation and exhalation I have come to appreciate the essence of diagonal reading and realise that I too frequently flick through the pages of long novels doing a skewed probe I've recalled the method employed by Oleg Sus of Brno who read all the literature and manuscripts that reached him like that and convinced myself that neither my eyes nor my mind need punctuation realised that not only I but hundreds of thousands of readers of newspapers and bestsellers not to mention the bureaucrats in high places forced to read kilograms of pages daily we can all turn a page a minute without losing the thread of a text's semantic message making diagonal reading a kind of suspended descent of the eyes from top to bottom though the alert mind always spots where to pause in this kind of reading because a higher signalling system says that here is something worthy of the reader's attention here he must revert for a tiny moment to horizontal reading as if to underline in red a core message and then carry on in the manner of alert subliminal global reading [...] ...by that same method I select from my past those buried images that so surprise me like Dadaist sentences and words pulled out of a surrealist hat [...] ...by reading diagonally a reader finds only imprints of himself but also what structures the style of the person who wrote the text...[126]

Leaving aside the fact that at the age of seventy Hrabal accepts with understanding and without protest the hurried way in which people today read, this text is pre-eminently evidence of his full awareness that skipping about or leaving bits out can do his writing no harm. Of the essence, however, is something else: Hrabal is here expressly handing part of his authorial competence – selecting buried images from the past – to the reader. Let the reader decide for himself, by his "diagonal reading", what he wants to be gripped and surprised by. Let the reader make his personal selection from within the text (also allowing for chance to work for him) and complete the work by comparing and contrasting it with his own life experience.

126) *Vita Nuova*, in *SSBH*, Vol. 11, pp. 181–82 (trans. DS, because here Tony Liman's version is greatly abridged.)

That such reader collaboration is genuinely being reckoned with is also attested by sentences in *Gaps* placed in the mouth of Hrabal's wife:

> So I say, Mother, I can't believe it, I looked at that famous book of his, but when I read it, I got the sense that every reader should finish it off at home, that with my husband's writing it's like those prepared meals I buy, the ones I have to finish off, tweak a bit, add spice to so they're whole...[127]

The rawness, plotlessness, undisciplined composition, anacolutha and rule-averse phrasing of sentences are all, to Hrabal's way of thinking, a challenge to readers: it all acquires order only in a private, dynamic reconstruction of the author's "style structure".

127) *Gaps*, p. 12.

X

The definitive version of *Gaps,* the last part of the trilogy, was completed in December 1985. A year later, Hrabal published his collection of autobiographical prose pieces *Život bez smokingu* (Life Without a Dinner Jacket). It included *inter alia* three prime, lengthier texts written during the first half of the 1980s: 'Autíčko' (Toy car), a "ballad" about the trials and tribulations of living with cats (in Hrabal, the life of animals is never separated from the lives of people), another reminiscence on Vladimír Boudník, 'Dandy v montérkách' (A Dandy in Dungarees), and the powerful confession 'Kdo jsem' (Who I am). These are all written in the same lyrically rhythmical sentences, though this time without the tender heart of the female voice. The narratorial perspective has changed: now the speaker is Hrabal himself.

The circle of Hrabal's work had begun to close. In these late texts, an author who had once turned his back on lyrical soliloquy to become the mirror of others' faces and recorder of what others say, who in later works hid behind the characters whose stories he was telling, and who finally, with diffidence, took his portrait from the viewpoint of his wife, now took back the floor in order to speak only for and about himself.

In 1987 Hrabal's brother Slávek and his wife Eliška both died, and a year later Karel Marysko. For a time Hrabal fell silent. He returned to writing only late in 1988, encouraged by the interest of a circle of young people that had sprung up around him and who eventually took charge of editing and publishing his writings. Key among them was Václav Kadlec and his publishing house Pražská imaginace, which, after the "velvet" revolution, published the nineteen-volume, meticulously edited *Collected Works.* Hrabal described his last texts, written between 1988 and 1995, as "literary journalism", though we might use the term Hrabal once used himself as he took down Uncle Pepin's monologues, "transcription". For these are "transcripts" of a sort, recording his meditations on growing old, the burden of loneliness, thoughts of suicide, his literary loves, his trip to America, but also on the changed political scene after the fall of communism. Like the erstwhile records of Pepin's ramblings, these records, too, are often of a "pre-literary" nature.

Kadlec's Pražská imaginace published these texts immediately after they were written as offprints for the benefit of Hrabal's circle of admirers, then they gradually appeared in a number of collections in book form: *Listopadový uragán* (November hurricane, 1990), *Ponorné říčky* (Subterranean streams, 1991), *Růžový kavalír* (Rosenkavalier, 1991), *Aurora na mělčině* (Aurora on a sandbank, 1992) and *Večerníčky pro Cassia* (Bedtime stories for Cassius, 1993). The series was rounded off with *Texty* (Texts, 1994), edited by Tomáš Mazal. These collections are distinctly uneven as to their merit. In them, Hrabal had given up on all literary conventions, all literary *bienséance*, for good: there is in them much repetition, pap, naïvité and the (sometimes quite amusing) posturing of an old man. Some of the late prose, such as *Kouzelná flétna* (Magic flute), *Totální strachy* (Total fears), *Aurora on a Sandbank*, *Ubili koníčka ubili* (They Killed the Little Horse, They Did), are nevertheless instances of a remarkably concentrated, merciless, existential vivisection possessed of a – to use Hrabal's favourite adjective – "wounding" eloquence.

My daily coming to, and my daily two cigarettes and a vitamin drink, and my daily descent in the lift and my daily bus ride from Sokolniků to the Dike of Eternity, where I lived daily for near on twenty years, and my shopping trips to fast food places to get stuff for the cats and cans of daily milk, and my daily being awaited by my cats by the Footbridge and my daily... etc. ... don't exactly make me a wiser man, but I can see perfectly well the slippage of the aura that I have created around myself and that has now gone flying down into the mud... once, my halo being no longer, it was through literature that I shoved a burning fag-end in my ear and now smouldering inside my head is the incipient legacy from my mother, a tender softening of the brain... But can that be helped? Even my daily doses of sedatives and late-afternoon doses of beer... that's just putting things off till night-time, when I do fall asleep, but towards dawn I get woken by delirifacient images that go on and that I look forward to, despite dreading them. Before dawn I'm always that table with the legs missing...[128]

---

128) *Ubili koníčka ubili*, in *SSBH*, Vol. 14, pp. 222–44 (236)

Here Hrabal is speaking from the position of an old man who has "achieved the acme of vacuity".[129] Coaxed into it by an American specialist in Czech studies, he undertook a round trip of US universities, where he once more adopted the role of "writer", but in the later texts he says very little about his writing. It is clear that he senses that he is losing that faculty for amazement that had once been the wellspring of his creativity.

In the confessional "transcripts", we are being addressed not by a writer, but by a careworn old man who knows that he is losing the aura of his talent for yarn-spinning. In vain would we seek here anything like his writer's creed. To hear anything of the kind, we must go back to *Vita nuova,* the work in which his return to himself was effectively completed:

> At first there's astonishment but then you begin to analyze which in turn leads to a remoteness a certain passivity but not to worry that's nothing but humility a spark of anticipation a moment prior to the holy announcement when your eyes are wide open and your soul is wide open and suddenly the passivity is turned on its head and it's not just that you *want* to take it all down you *must* take it all down and a writer is one who transcribes what he has seen what has been revealed and the whole thing is a huge kick in the pants knowing there's something out there other than yourself...[130]

---

129) One of Hrabal's favourite ideas, with an allusion to Taoism. See, for example, *Too Loud a Solitude*, in *SSBH*, Vol. 9, p. 36.
130) *Vita nuova*, p. 14.

SSBH = Hrabal Bohumil, *Sebrané spisy* 1-19, edited by Miroslav Červenka, Karel Dostál, Vladimír Gardavský, Milada Chlíbcová, Jaroslava Janáčková, Milan Jankovič, Václav Kadlec, Claudio Poeta and Jiřina Zumrová. Prague: Pražská imaginace, 1992-96

Poupata = Hrabal, Bohumil: *Poupata,* Prague: Mladá fronta, 1970

Černý, Václav, 'Za hádankami Bohumila Hrabala, pokus interpretační' (1975), in: *Eseje o české a slovenské próze.* Prague: Torst, 1994, pp. 89-133.

Drozda, Miroslav: 'Hrabalův mýtus a děj', in: Milan Jankovič and Josef Zumr: *Hrabaliana.* Prague: Prostor, 1990, pp. 89-94.

Frynta, Emanuel: 'Náčrt základů Hrabalovy prózy', in: Bohumil Hrabal: *Automat Svět. Výbor povídek.* Prague: Mladá fronta, 1966, pp. 312-331.

Jankovič, Milan: *Kapitoly z poetiky Bohumila Hrabala.* Prague: Torst, 1996.

Lopatka, Jan: *Předpoklady tvorby. Výběr kritických článků a recenzí z let 1965-1969.* Prague: Československý spisovatel, 1991.

Roth, Susanne: *Laute Einsamkeit und bitteres Glück. Zur poetischen Welt von Bohumil Hrabals Prosa.* Berne etc.: Peter Lang [Slavica Helvetica], 1986.

Short, David (ed.): *Bohumil Hrabal (1914-97). Papers from a Symposium.* London: School of Slavonic and East European Studies, University College London, 2004.

Todorov, Tzvetan: *Poétique de la prose.* Paris: Seuil, 1978.

Much has been written on Hrabal's death, but the reader may care to find the long (nearly 2,500 wds) piece by Alexander Kaczorowski: 'The Mysterious Death of Bohumil Hrabal (1914-1997)'. *Aspen Review*, 2013/4 https://www.aspen.review/aspen-review

This essay originated as the foreword to a wide-ranging Hrabal anthology *(Opere scelte)* compiled by two leading Italian authorities on the Czech writer, Annalisa Cosentino and Sergio Corduas, and published in 2003 by Mondadori in Milan within its prestigious series "I Meridiani". An expanded version in Czech under the title *Bohumil Hrabal: pokus o portrét* (BH: a trial portrait) had been published a year earlier by Torst in Prague. In a slightly revised form it reappeared in my *Kapitoly z francouzské, italské a české literatury* (Chapters from French, Italian and Czech literature; Prague: Karolinum, 2007, pp. 404–466), to be republished a third time, again by Torst, in 2015.

There are several reasons why I was so seized with this task. The first is the most personal: my abiding love for Bohumil Hrabal and above all the fact that he was the one Czech author whose 'literary fate' I was able to follow first-hand from first book to last. And then there was the seemingly extraneous reason in the form of the monumental edition of Hrabal's *Collected Works*, published by Václav Kadlec's Pražská imaginace, which gave me an opportunity, nay, in light of the above, the duty, to re-read Hrabal again.

The bibliography includes only those works that are cited directly, though my debt to the vast literature on Hrabal is undoubtedly greater. The outstanding monographs by Susanna Roth and Milan Jankovič so far constitute the foundations for any consideration of the writer that they amount very largely to a genuine palimpsest of the present book (and, I am sure, of any future writings on Hrabal). I cannot, however, preclude a measure of debt to works that I have taken to stand aside from my own view of Hrabal. I have only attempted two things herein: to slot Hrabal's work more systematically into the European context and to place more emphasis on the thematic elements within its overall structure.

Today, the reader will find a detailed bibliography of books, articles and reviews to go with each separate item in the new series of Hrabal's Writings (*Spisy*), edited by Václav Kadlec and Jiří Pelán and published in seven volumes by Mladá fronta in Prague during 2014–2019. Below we list just the most important contributions in languages other than Czech.

J. P.

SELECT INTERNATIONAL BIBLIOGRAPHY

Baluch, Jacek: *Kain wedlug Hrabala*, Cracow: Wydawnictwo «Scriptum», 2007.

Catalano, Alessandro: Bohumil Hrabal. From "The Pearls on the Bottom" to "Total Fears". *The Prague Revue*, 1998, No. 5, pp. 75–91.

Catalano, Alessandro: Bohumil Hrabal, in: Catalano, Alessandro: *Sole rosso su Praga. La letteratura ceca fra socialismo e underground (1945-1959)*, Rome: Bulzoni 2004, pp. 245–270.

Cosentino, Annalisa: Ritagli, in: Bohumil Hrabal, *Sanguinose ballate e miracolose leggende*, Rome: Edizioni e/o, 1998, pp. 207–217.

Cosentino, Annalisa (ed.): *Intorno a Bohumil Hrabal.* Atti dcl Convegno intermazionale di studi, Udine 27–29 ottobre 2005, Udine: Forum Editrice, 2006.

Češka, Jakub: Ironiczna bezdomność Bohumila Hrabala i tlumiona tesknota za domem Milana Kundery, *Porównania*, 2012, No. 11, pp. 87-99.

Engelking, Leszek: Nadrealny realizm, in: Engelking, Leszek: *Surrealizm, underground, postmodernizm: Szkice o literaturze czeskiej*, Łódź: Wydawnictwo uniwersytetu Łódzkiego, 2001, pp. 103–106.

Galmiche, Xavier: Altérité et aliénation chez Bohumil Hrabal, in: Bechtel, Delphine (ed.): *Figures du marginal dans les littératures centro-européennes,* Paris: UFR d'Etudes germaniques, Université Paris Sorbonne, 2001, pp. 49–65.

Galmiche, Xavier, De Préval, Jitka, Stránská, Lenka (eds): *Bohumil Hrabal, le palabreur.* Paris: Centre tchèque – Université Paris Sorbonne, 2001.

Galmiche, Xavier, Maréchal, André (eds): Bohumil Hrabal. Palabres et existence, Paris: Presses de l'Université Paris-Sorbonne, 2002.

Gibian, George: The Haircutting and I Waited on the King of England: Two Recent Works by Bohumil Hrabal, in: Harkins, William E., Trensky, Paul I. (eds), *Czech Literature since 1936: A Symposium*, New York: Columbia Slavic Studies, 1980, pp. 74-90.

Götz, Alexander: *Bilder aus der Tiefe der Zeit. Erinnerung und Selbststilisierung als ästhctische Funktionen im Werk Bohumil Hrabals*, Frankfurt a. M.: P. Lang, 1998.

Goszczyńska, Joanna (ed.): *W poszukiwaniu przerw w zabudowie*, Warszawa: Wydzial polonistyki UW, 2015.

Greene, Richard Allen: The fears of a literary immortality, *The Prague Post*, 8, 24.-30. 6. 1998, No. 25, p. 4.

Jamek, Václav: Pour le Néant de Dieu, in: Bohumil Hrabal, *Une trop bruyante solitude*, Paris: Seuil, 1997, pp. I–XI.

James, Petra: *Bohumil Hrabal: "Composer un monde blessant à coups de ciseaux et de gomme arabique"*, Paris: Classiques Garnier, 2013.

Kaczorowski, Aleksander: *Gra w żicie. Opowieść o Bohumilu Hrabalu*, Wolowiec: Czarne, 2004.

Kardyni-Pelikánová, Krystyna: Ocalić podmiotowość. Para-epistolarne formy w polskiej i czeskiej prozie wspólczesnej (na przykladzie "Listów do Jerzego" M. Kuncewiczowej i "Huraganu listopadowego" B. Hrabala), *Litteraria Humanitas*, Vol. 4, 1996, pp. 409–426.

Kunstmann, Heinrich: Zur auditiven Stilisierung in der modernen tschechischen Prosa: John, Hašek, Hrabal, *Die Welt der Slawen*, 1970, pp. 363–387.

Mercks, Kees: The Landscape in Harlequin's millions, in: Haard, Eric de, Honselaar, Wim (eds): *Literature and Beyond. Festschrift for Willem G. Weststeijn*, Amsterdam: Pegasus, 2008, pp. 419–435.

Meyer, Holt: Roland Barthes's Masks in Bohumil Hrabal's Gaps: Acounts of a Transfer, Transfer of Accounts, *Slovo a smysl*, 2015, No. 24, pp. 59–89.

Pelán, Jiří: Bohumil Hrabal e la Mitteleuropa, in: Rónaky, Eszter, Tombi, Beáta (eds): *Dal centro dell'Europa. Culture a confronto tra Trieste e Carpazi. Atti del Secondo seminario interdisciplinare*, Pécs, 26.–29. 9. 2002, Pécs: Imago mundi, 2002, pp. 57–64.

Pilař, Martin: Hrabal and Boudník – the Fatal Friendship, in: *Sborník prací filozofické fakulty Ostravské univerzity. Literární věda*, 1997, No. 3, pp. 51–57.

Ripellino, Angelo Maria: Introduzione, in: Bohumil Hrabal: *Inserzione per una casa in cui non voglio piu abitare*, Turin: Einaudi 1968, pp. 7–12.

Roth, Susanna: „Mrtvomat". Montáž – Die erste literarische Collage Bohumil Hrabals, in: Brang, Peter, Nivat, George, Zett, Robert (eds): *Schweizerische Beiträge zum IX. Internationalen Slavistenkongress in Kiev*, Bern – Frankfurt a. M. – New York: Peter Lang, 1983, pp. 193–218.

Roth, Susanna: *Laute Einsamkeit und bitteres Glück. Zur poetischen Welt von Bohumil Hrabals Prosa*, Bern: Peter Lang, 1986.

Roth, Susanna: *Hommage à Hrabal*, Frankfurt a. M.: Suhrkamp, 1989.

Salmon, Christian: *A bâtons rompus avec Bohumil Hrabal*, Paris: Criterion, 1991.

Short, David (ed.): *Bohumil Hrabal (1914–97). Papers from a Symposium*, London: University College London, School of Slavonic and East European Studies, 2004.

Slavíčková, Miloslava: *Bohumil Hrabals litterära collage*, Lund: Lund University Department of East and Central European Studies, 2003.

Soliński, Wojciech: *Bohumila Hrabala sprawa polska (i inne sprawy)*, Wroclaw: ATUT, 2013.

Stanzel, Elisabeth: Tanzstunden für Erwachsene und Fortgeschrittene, *Forum. Österreichische Monatsblätter für kulturelle Freiheit*, 12, 1965, No. 144, pp. 585–586.

Stolz-Hladká, Zuzana: Bohumil Hrabal and the Corporeality of the World, in: Sériot, Patrick (ed.): *Contributions suisses au XIIIe Congrès International des Slavistes à Ljubljana*, Bern: P. Lang, 2003, pp. 305–324.

Škvorecký, Josef: American Motifs in the Work of Bohumil Hrabal, *Cross Currents*, 1982, No. 1, pp. 207–218.

Špirit, Michael: *Bohumil Hrabal: una sfida per storici ed editori*, Udine: Forum Editrice, 2003.

Urbaszewski, Laura Shear: Rethinking the Grotesque in Hrabal's Fiction: Carnival as a Model for Closely Watched Trains, *Brown Slavic Contributions. Modern Czech Studies*, Vol. 13, 2000, pp. 34–46.

Wood, James: Bohumil Hrabal, *London Review of Books*, Vol. 23, No. 1, 2001, pp. 14–16.

At Polná, 1917

Between his stepfather Francin and his mother and brother Břetislav in the early 1920s

With brother Břetislav, 1922

In the early 1930s

In 1935

Vlastnoruční podpis majitele:

Bohumil Hrabal

Akademický slib vykonán.

25. ŘÍJ 1939
ABS...ORIUM
...A 178 ai 1939/40.

SEZNAM PŘEDNÁŠEK,
(INDEX LECTIONUM)

do kterých byl zapsán
jako řádný posluchač
(quas se frequentaturum rite professus est).

Bohumil Hrabal

Rodiště (oriundus): *Brno — Židenice*

Otec (pater): *František Hrabal*

Zapsán na fakultě
(Inscriptio in facultate)

právnické

UNIVERSITY KARLOVY V PRAZE,
(Universitatis Carolinae Pragensis)

Dne (die)

kvestor (quaestor).

Student record book, 1935

The young gentleman from the brewery in the 1930s

In Brno in the second half of the 1930s

On leave from military service in 1946

With his uncle Josef Hrabal – known as 'Pepin' – in the early 1930s

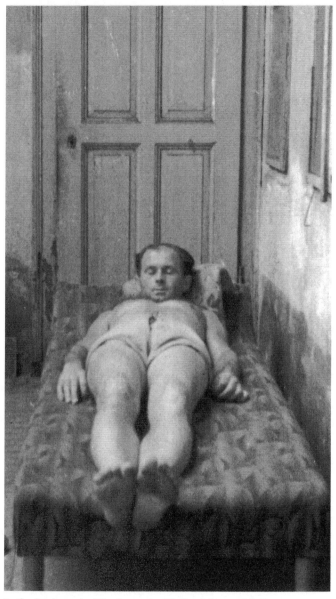

In the back yard of the house in Libeň while on sick leave
following his accident at the Kladno steelworks in 1952

In the mid-1950s

On National Avenue (Národní třída), Prague, 1955

With Eliška Plevová – 'Pipsi' at Libeň in 1956

Outside the scrap paper recycling facility at 10 Spálená St., Prague, in 1956.
Photo: Jiří Kolář

With the Grundza sisters and Bob the dog, Libeň, 1957

At 24 Na Hrázi St., Libeň, in the 1950s. Photo: Emanuel Frynta

Josef Hrabal – 'Pepin' – in Nymburk, 1957. Photo: Jiří Kolář

Taking a shower, 1957

During his tour of the USA as a writer in 1964

Outside 24 Na Hrázi St., Libeň, in 1965. Photo: Václav Chochola

Eliška Plevová – 'Pipsi' – outside 24 Na Hrázi St., Libeň, in 1965.
Photo: Václav Chochola

At 24 Na Hrázi St., Libeň, in 1969. Photo: Jan Reich

		Příjmení a jméno	HRABAL Bohumil
	Členská legitimace		laureát státní ceny K.g.
	SVAZU		
	ČESKÝCH		
	SPISOVATELŮ	Adresa	PRAHA 8 - Libeň
			Na Hrázi 24
Podpis majitele			
Vystavena 24. 3. 70 předseda SČS		Datum narození	28. března 1914
číslo 152			Brno - Židenice

Union of Czech Writers membership card bearing the signature of Jaroslav Seifert, Union chairman and Nobel prize-winner, 1970

At Holešovice cemetery after his hospitalisation, 1973. Photo: Ladislav Michálek

In a cafeteria in Myslíkova St., Prague, 1978. Photo: Milan Jankovič

At Kersko in the late 1970s. Photo: Milan Jankovič

At Kersko in the 1980s.

At Kersko, 1988. Photo: Milan Jankovič

At Kersko, 1994. Photo: Tomáš Mazal

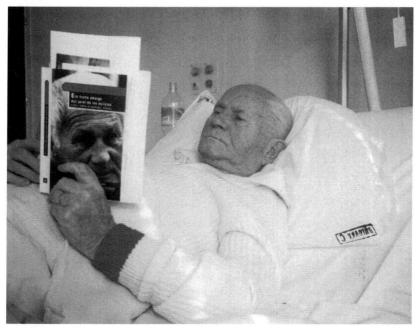

In his Bulovka hospital bed in January 1997. Photo: Tomáš Mazal

Unless stated otherwise, the photos are drawn from the author's own archive.

While I have obviously sought to be true to the author's text, I have also tried to be true to his intent, namely the desire to bring a better knowledge of Bohumil Hrabal and his works to a wider foreign, specifically an Anglo-Saxon readership, rather than solely to an audience of scholars. Thus I have taken some liberties with the 'high' terminology, I have made some non-obtrusive insertions to expand on certain words or references that are plain to a Czech readership, but certainly less so to the foreign reader, and in other circumstances I have resorted to footnotes for similar reasons. Footnotes that are mine, as opposed to those adopted from the author's original text (in which they were mostly references in brackets, not 'below the line') are marked [DS].

The work discusses huge numbers of Hrabal's works, which raises the problem of titling. In the vast majority of cases, I have kept the original title at its first occurrence, followed immediately by a translation in brackets, then at every subsequent mention of the same work, I have used the English translation of its title only. Just occasionally there will acknowledgment of the existence of more than one title in translation.

Many of Hrabal's works have never been translated, so my suggested English titles are entirely provisional. In the case of works that have been previously published in English translation I have kept to that 'established' title (footnoting any misgivings about them as applicable). All the passages quoted from individual works are given here in English only: where a published translation exists (and has been accessible), I have used quotations from them; where no translation exists (the majority), where the existing translation is from a different version of the original work, or where it does not match the excerpt requiring translation (for instance, because it has been abridged for reasons best known to the translator), the translations are mine – with the hope that they will pass muster.

I have also adopted the usual British convention of giving titles of whole works in italics, those of part works in roman, within single inverted commas. Occasionally there may be some ambiguity depending on what 'variant or variation' of a text is meant.

Another addition that I have made to the text is the inclusion of one or two English-language (and so accessible) references to sources that do not figure in the Literature listed in the Czech version of this book.

Finally, I have created an index of names and a would-be complete list of translations of Hrabal's works into English (some small number may prove in time to have been omitted, whether by my oversight or their irretrievability).

All of the above interventions and conventions have been done with the agreement and understanding of the author.

David Short
(Windsor, January 2019)

UK and US editions are listed separately, since it is not always apparent whether, in some cases, items are or are not merely local mutations of one and the same thing.

A) Czech > English

'Autíčko' (first in a Czech compilation *Život bez smokingu*, Praha: Československý spisovatel, 1986) as *All My Cats*. Translated by Paul Wilson. New York: New Directions, 2019.

Automat svět, as *The Death of Mr. Baltisberger*. Translated by Michael Henry Heim, Introduction by Daniel S. Miritz (translated by Káča Poláčková). London: Sphere Books (Abacus), 1966; New York: Bantam Doubleday Dell, 1973; New York: Doubleday & Company, 1975.

The stories in this English compilation are not quite a complete version of the Czech compilation published as *Automat svět*. It contains: **'Rukověť pábitelského učně'** (as *Handbook for the Apprentic Palaverer*), **'Romance'** (*Romance*), **'Pábitelé'** (*Palaverers*), **'Andělské voči'** (*Angel Eyes*), **'Fádní odpoledne'** (*A Dull Afternoon*), **'Večerní kurs'** (*Evening Course*), **'Pohřeb'** (*The Funeral*), **'Pan notář'** (*The Notary*), **'U zeleného stromu'** (*At the Sign of the Greentree*), **'Diamantové očko'** (*Diamond Eye*), **'Pražské jesličky'** (*A Prague Nativity*), **'Emánek'** (*Little Eman*), **'Smrt pana Baltisbergra'** (*The Death of Mr Baltisberger*), **'Automat svět'** (*The World Cafeteria*) and **'Chcete vidět Zlatou Prahu?'** (*Want to see Golden Prague?*). Many of these stories had appeared earlier in the other collections, **Perlička na dně** (*Pearls of the Deep*) and **Pábitelé** (*Palaverers*), as indeed follows from the book.

'Automat svět', as 'The World Cafeteria'. Translated by Jeanne W. Němcová, in *Czech and Slovak Short Stories* (ed. J. W. Němcová). London, New York: Oxford University Press, 1967, pp. 136–149.

Dopisy Dubence, as *Total Fears. Letters to Dubenka*. [A Selection] Translated by James Naughton. Prague: Twisted Spoon Press, 1998.

This selection from the far more numerous 'letters' contains **'Kouzelná flétna'** (*The Magic Flute*), **'Veřejná sebevražda'** (*Public Suicide*), **'Pár vět'** (*A Few Sentences*), **'Bílý kůň'** (*The White Horse*), **'Listopadový uragán'** (*November Hurricane*), **'Mešuge stunde'** (*Meshuge Stunde*), **'Že jsme radši nevyhořeli'** (*A Pity We Didn't Burn to Death Instead*), **'Totální strachy'** (*Total Fears*) and **'Růžový kavalír'** (*The Rosenkavalier*).

Harlekýnovy milióny, as *Harlequin's Millions: A Fairy Tale*. Translated by Stacey Knecht. Brooklyn NY: Archipelago Books, 2014.

Inzerát na dům, ve kterém už nechci bydlet, as *Mr. Kafka and Other Tales from the Time of the Cult*. Translated by Paul Wilson. New York: New Directions, 2015.

'*Kafkárna*', as 'The Kafkorium', Translated by W. L. Solberg, in **New Writing of East Europe** (eds. George Gömöri and Charles Newman). Chicago: Quadrangle Books, 1968, pp. 179–189.

Kličky na kapesníku. Román-interview (ptal se a odpovědi zaznamenal László Szigeti), as *Pirouettes on a Postage Stamp: an interview-novel with questions asked and answers recorded by Laszlo Szigeti*. Translated, with an Introduction and notes, by David Short. Prague: Karolinum, 2008.

'*Kresba*', as 'Drawing' (a poem from the 1939 MS collection *Dny a noci* [Days and Nights]). Translated by David Chirico and included in his paper: 'Towards a Typology of Hrabal's Intertextuality: Bohumil Hrabal and Giuseppe Ungaretti', in David Short (ed.): *Bohumil Hrabal (1914-97). Papers from a Symposium*. London: School of Slavonic and East European Studies, University College London, 2004, pp. 11–33 (18).

Městečko, kde se zastavil čas, as *The Little Town Where Time Stood Still* (published jointly with *Postřižiny*, see below). Translated by James Naughton, Introduction by Josef Škvorecký. London: Sphere Books (Abacus) and New York: Pantheon Books, 1993.

Městečko, kde se zastavil čas, as *The Little Town Where Time Stood Still*. Translated by James Naughton. Harmondsworth: Penguin (Penguin Modern Classics), 2017.

Něžný barbar, as *The Gentle Barbarian*. Translated by Paul Wilson, New York: New Directions, and London: Penguin, 2019.

Obsluhoval jsem anglického krále, as *I Served the King of England*. Translated by Paul Wilson. London: Chatto & Windus, 1989; London: Pan Books (Picador), 1990; New York: Harcourt Brace Jovanovich, 1989; New York: Vintage Books, 1990; New York: New Directions, 2007.

Obsluhoval jsem anglického krále, as *I Served the King of England*. Translated by Paul Wilson, Introduction by Adam Thirlwell. Harmondsworth: Penguin (Vintage Classics), 2009.

Ostře sledované vlaky, as *A Close Watch on the Trains*. Translated by Edith Pargeter. London: Jonathan Cape, 1968.

Ostře sledované vlaky, as *Closely Watched Trains*. Translated by Edith Pargeter. New York: Grove Press, 1968; Harmondsworth: Penguin, 1981.

Ostře sledované vlaky, as *Closely Watched Trains*. Translated by Edith Pargeter, Foreword by Josef Škvorecký. New York: Penguin Books, 1981; Evanston IL: Northwestern University Press, 1990.

Ostře sledované vlaky, as *Closely Observed Trains*. Translated by Edith Pargeter. London: Sphere Books (Abacus), 1990.

Ostře sledované vlaky, as *Closely Observed Trains: A Film by Jiří Menzel and Bohumil Hrabal*. Translated by Josef Holzbecher. London: Lorrimer Publishing, 1971; New York: Simon and Schuster, 1971.

'*Pábitelé*', as 'A Breath of Fresh Air'. Translated by Marian Wilbraham, in *Seven Short Stories*, Prague: Orbis, 1965, 1967, pp. 53–67.

'*Pábitelé*', as 'A Breath of Fresh Air'. Translated by Marian Wilbraham, in *New Writing in Czechoslovakia* (comp. George Theiner). Baltimore, Harmondsworth: Penguin, 1969, pp. 558–567.

Postřižiny, as *Cutting it Short* (published jointly with *Městečko, kde se zastavil čas*, see above). Translated by James Naughton, Introduction by Josef Škvorecký. London: Sphere Books (Abacus), 1993; New York: Pantheon Books, 1993.

Postřižiny, as *Cutting it Short*. Translated by James Naughton. Harmondsworth: Penguin (Penguin modern Classics), 2017.

Příliš hlučná samota, as *Too Loud a Solitude*. Translated by Michael Henry Heim, in **Cross-Currents: a Yearbook of Central European Culture** (Ann Arbor: Dept. of Slavic Languages and Literatures, University of Michigan), Vol. 5, 1986, pp. 279–332.

Příliš hlučná samota, as *Too Loud a Solitude*. Translated by Michael Henry Heim. London: Sphere Books (Abacus), 1990; London: Deutsch, 1991; San Diego, New York, London: Harcourt Brace Jovanovich, 1990, 1992.

Proluky, as *Gaps: A Novel*. Translated by Tony Liman, Evanston, IL: Northwestern University Press, 2011.

'*Scherzo*' (a poem published in **Občanské listy** in 1938). Translated by David Chirico and included in his paper: 'Towards a Typology of Hrabal's Intertextuality: Bohumil Hrabal and Giuseppe Ungaretti', in David Short (ed.): **Bohumil Hrabal (1914–97). Papers from a Symposium**. London: School of Slavonic and East European Studies, University College London, 2004, pp. 11–33 (23).

Rukověť pábitelského učně, as *Rambling On: An Apprentice's Guide to the Gift of the Gab*. Translated by David Short, Afterword by Václav Kadlec, Illustrations by Jiří Grus. Prague: Karolinum Press, 2014 (hbk); 2016[2] (pbk without illustrations). This modern edition, coinciding with Hrabal's original intention, overlaps in part the censored 1978 collection **Slavnosti sněženek** (The Snowdrop Festival).

This selection contains: '**Hostinec u Bernardýna**' (*The St Bernard Inn*), '**Měsičná noc**' (*A Moonlit Night*), '**Pan Metek**' (*Mr Methie*), '**Zdivočelá kráva**' (*A Feral Cow*), '**Králíčci v křídle**' (*A Grand Piano Rabbit Hutch*), '**Jumbo**', '**Mazánkův zázrak**' (*Mazánek's Wonder*), '**Slavnosti sněženek**

(*The Snowdrop Festival*), '**Přátelé**' (*Friends*), '**Školení**' (*Fining Salami*), '**Leli**', '**Beatrice**', '**Lucinka a Pavlína**' (*Lucy and Polly*), '**Hostina**' (*The Feast*), '**Pan Iontek**' (*Ionic Man*), '**Vlasy jako pivarník**' (*Hair Like Pivarník's*), '**Družička**' (*The Maid of Honour*), '**Adagio Lamentoso**', '**Rukověť pábitelského učně**' (*An Apprentice's Guide to the Gift of the Gab**).

Svatby v domě. Dívčí románek, as *In-house Weddings*. Translated by Tony Liman. Evanston IL: Northwestern University Press, 2007.

Taneční hodiny pro starší a pokročilé, as *Dancing Lessons for the Advanced in Age*. Translated by Michael Henry Heim. New York, San Diego, London: Harcourt Brace & Co., 1995.

Taneční hodiny pro starší a pokročilé, as *Dancing Lessons for the Advanced in Age*. Translated by Michael Henry Heim, with lithographs by Vladimir Suchanek. London: Harvill Press, 1998.

Taneční hodiny pro starší a pokročilé, as *Dancing Lessons for the Advanced in Age*. Translated by Michael Henry Heim. Harmondsworth: Penguin (Vintage Classics), 2009.

[The untitled 'introduction' or 'foreword' to] *toto město je ve společné péči obyvatel*, as *this city is in the joint care of its inhabitants*. Translated by David Short, In: David Short (ed.): *Bohumil Hrabal (1914-97). Papers from a Symposium*. London: School of Slavonic and East European Studies, University College London, 2004, Appendix 1, pp. 119-121; p. 70, fn. 1.

Vita nuova: Kartinky, as *Vita nuova: a novel*. Translated Tony Liman. Evanston, IL: Northwestern University Press, 2010.

---

* The work known elsewhere as 'A handbook for the Apprentice Palaverer' (Heim).

B) English > Czech

This is a complete list of the English titles of whole books or part-works (single poems or stories), cross-referred to section **A**. The list is alphabetical by the first main word, i.e. it ignores 'A(n)' and 'The', and by the English alphabet.

'Adagio Lamentoso' – see under ***Rukověť pábitelského učně***

'All My Cats' - see under ***'Autíčko'***

'Angel' – see under ***Inzerát na dům, ve kterém už nechci bydlet***

'Angel Eyes' – see under ***Automat svět***

'An Apprentice's guide to the Gift of the Gab' – see under ***Rukověť pábitelského učně***

'At the Sign of the Greentree' – see under ***Automat svět***

'Beatrice' – see under ***Rukověť pábitelského učně***

'Beautiful Poldi' – see under ***Inzerát na dům, ve kterém už nechci bydlet***

'A Betrayal of Mirrors' – see under ***Inzerát na dům, ve kterém už nechci bydlet***

'Breaking Through the Drum' – see under ***Inzerát na dům, ve kterém už nechci bydlet***

'A Breath of Fresh Air' – see under ***'Pábitelé'***

A Close Watch on the Trains – see ***Ostře sledované vlaky***

Closely Observed Trains – see ***Ostře sledované vlaky***

Closely Observed Trains: A Film... – see ***Ostře sledované vlaky***

Closely Watched Trains – see ***Ostře sledované vlaky***

Cutting it Short – see ***Postřižiny***

Dancing Lessons for the Advanced in Age – see ***Taneční hodiny pro starší a pokročilé***

'The Death of Mr Baltisberger' – see under ***Automat svět***

'Diamond Eye' – see under ***Automat svět***

'Drawing' – see ***'Kresba'***

'A Dull Afternoon' – see under ***Automat svět***

'Evening Course' – see under ***Automat svět***

'The Feast' – see under ***Rukověť pábitelského učně***

'A Feral Cow' – see under ***Rukověť pábitelského učně***

'A Few Sentences' – see under ***Dopisy Dubence***

'Fining Salami' – see under ***Rukověť pábitelského učně***

'Friends' – see under ***Rukověť pábitelského učně***

'The Funeral' – see under ***Automat svět***

Gaps: A Novel – see ***Proluky***

The Gentle Barbarian – see ***Něžný barbar***

'A Grand Piano Rabbit Hutch' – see under ***Rukověť pábitelského učně***

'Total Fears' – see under ***Dopisy Dubence***

Vita nuova: a novel – see ***Vita nuova. Kartinky***

'Want to see Golden Prague?' – see under ***Automat svět***

'The White Horse' – see under ***Dopisy Dubence***

'The World Cafeteria' – see (tr. Michael Henry Heim) under ***Automat svět***, and (tr. Jeanne W. Němcová) **'*Automat svět*'**

INDEX OF NAMES

The inclusion of this list is based on the assumption that while readers of the book will have been *a priori* familiar with the name of Hrabal himself, many of the other Czech names mentioned will be less than familiar to the broader English-speaking readership. For further reading, note that almost all are covered by quite reasonable English-language Wikipedia pages. (Page references in italics apply to footnotes.)